Creative Educational Leadership

ALSO AVAILABLE FROM CONTINUUM

9 Habits of Highly Effective Teachers, Jacquie Turnbull

Rethinking Educational Leadership, John West-Burnham

School and System Leadership, Susan Robinson

Creative
Educational
Leadership

A Practical Guide to Leadership as Creativity

JACQUIE TURNBULL

B L O O M S B U R Y
LONDON · NEW DELHI · NEW YORK · SYDNEY

Bloomsbury Academic
An imprint of Bloomsbury Publishing Plc

50 Bedford Square	175 Fifth Avenue
London	New York
WC1B 3DP	NY 10010
UK	USA

www.bloomsbury.com

First published 2012

© Jacquie Turnbull, 2012

ISBN: PB: 978-1-4411-6774-3
      ePub: 978-1-4411-9563-0
      PDF: 978-1-4411-7211-2

British Library Cataloguing-in-Publication Data
A catalogue record for this book is available from the British Library.

Library of Congress Cataloging-in-Publication Data
Smith, John
Title/John Smith p.cm
Includes bibliographic references and index.
ISBN 978-1-0000-1111-0 (hardcover) – ISBN 978-1-1111-0000-1 (pbk.)
2012045678

Typeset by Fakenham Prepress Solutions, Fakenham, Norfolk NR21 8NN
Printed and bound in India

In Memory of Elizabeth Newton
A creative teacher who taught from the heart

Contents

Acknowledgments

Extract from Trowler, P. (2002) *Education Policy: A policy sociology approach* 2nd Edn, pp. 115–17, London: RoutledgeFalmer.
Reproduced by kind permission of the publisher Taylor & Francis Books (UK),

I've often said there are similarities in writing a book to having a baby.

After the initial inspiration, there's a very long period of gestation, followed by a great deal of hard work. Finally, when production is achieved, you want to bask in admiring comments – you want people to say how lovely it is, and doesn't it smell nice!

Unlike delivering a baby, however, this book has benefited from the attention of many midwives. It has been sourced from the creative ideas of others gleaned from conversations, discussions and interviews.

Conversations shared with others formed my ideas, and I'm grateful for the helpful insights gained from Gary Brace, Nigel Brown, Peter Dolan, Sheila Drayton, Gerald Dunning, Paul Egan, Ann George, John Graystone, Wendy Jordan, Rob Larkins, Rachael Lucking and Kevin Pascoe.

The themes of the book were derived from interviews with individuals who demonstrate creative leadership in their own domain. Without exception, they responded readily to my request to interview them, and were unfailingly generous with their time and in sharing their experiences. Without their contribution the book could not have been created. In deference to those who wished to retain anonymity, I have used only first names throughout: however, they know who they are, and I can only repeat my gratitude for allowing me to draw on their expertise: Anthony – College Lecturer, David – Director of an Institute for Applied Education Research, Dick – Further Education College Principal, Gloria – Her Majesty's Inspectorate of Education lead inspector, Gordon – Research and consultancy company Director, Janet – Primary School Teacher, Kay – Further Education College Faculty Director, Mal – Secondary School Headteacher, Maria – Further Education College Faculty Head, Paul – Health Service Director, Paul – Consultant on complexity theory and leadership, Richard – Primary Headteacher, Sheelagh – Health Service Director.

When Headteacher Mal retired, he was fond of paraphrasing Isaac

Newton in claiming his successful career had been due to the fact that he had 'stood on the shoulders of giants'. No creation comes from nothing, and this book has similarly relied upon the substantial body of work of academics, researchers and writers, and most importantly, creative practitioners. I have endeavoured to be scrupulous in acknowledging their original work accurately, and I hope that they and others will accept my sincere thanks under this general rubric.

A particular mention for Anna Fleming and Rosie Pattinson at Bloomsbury for their professional support and patient assistance. And as always, special thanks to my family for their support and interest, and for keeping me grounded in reality.

I do not believe the above comes close to acknowledging all of the debts owed. So many people have contributed to this book, whether they know it or not, and I hope others not named will identify with my overall expression of sincere gratitude.

Introduction: The case for creativity

May you live in interesting times

ANCIENT CHINESE CURSE

You may read the saying above with a wry smile and recognize its truth. There is no doubt that we live through times that are challenging economically, socially and culturally, and none of us are immune to the changes that are being wrought.

Education may feel the impact of these changes more than any other sector. For some, a particular change is no less than a revolution: for writer on creativity Anna Craft, creativity has moved from the fringes to become a core aspect of education.[1]

Leadership at work also seems to have attained a higher profile over the last couple of decades. The guiding beacon of management theory seems to have dimmed, perhaps because it was inadequate anyway to chart a way through the shifting sands of a complex, ever-changing, global working environment. On the other hand, Rodney Ogawa and Steven Bossert think that this is nothing new, that leadership has always had a focal importance:

'There are concepts in our society on which much seems to turn. Because they are important, we look for them in special places. Leadership, it seems, is such a concept. It is important, most would agree.'[2]

So for this book I've brought together these two concepts of creativity and leadership because of their crucial importance to education in particular. But this is not a book about theorizing or attempting to define two complex and elusive concepts. Rather, I take the view that successful leaders in education already *are* creative. They juggle a host of variables; they find innovative solutions to problems others find intractable; they stimulate and motivate teachers and students to achieve their potential. So how do they do it? This book will attempt to discern the elements of creativity in how successful leaders do what they do.

In the world in general, creativity is no longer confined to activities of a broadly artistic nature. In education, creativity has cast away the taint associated with the chaotic and undisciplined approach of dramatic instances of failure of some schools in the 1960s. Creativity has emerged to be championed as beneficial for economies, for business and for society in general. In education, we have seen creativity break from the boundaries of artistic subjects to become a cross-curricular thinking skill, with the recognition that 'creative teaching' and 'teaching for creativity' are pedagogical skills applicable to all subjects. Indeed, passionate advocate Sir Ken Robinson claims that creativity is the new literacy.

Leadership also has been evolving. It's a feature of our modern world that the demands of leadership have increased, both in respect of handling complexity and keeping up with the rapid pace of change. Yet we can probably still say that we know effective leadership when we see it: we recognize leadership by the results leaders achieve; by the fact that the organization they lead is uniquely successful in their own field, or when they take a failing organisation and transform it into one that achieves unprecedented outcomes. Even so, as we seek to define leadership, it seems to slip further from our grasp: to become infinitely more complex and elusive. Academics have theorised, researchers have delved into every aspect and there must have been a million words written attempting to grasp the core essence of leadership.

On the one hand, the evolution has recognized leadership ability is not unique or restricted to a person in a leadership role. Rather, 'distributed leadership' is seen as a way of coping with the complexity of modern organizations, and policy makers are calling for leadership capacity and expertise to be nurtured within education communities.

Then there has been the growth of the 'personal' element, with Peter Senge suggesting that if you want to be a leader, you have to be a real human being; you must understand yourself first. Yet other researchers are studying vision and charisma as elements of leadership, and there's a growing focus on the interpersonal, moral and spiritual features

With all these changes, it may seem that the traditional hierarchal style of leadership has lost its relevance in our modern world. For one thing, young people moving into employment today will belong to the fast expanding cohort that has been named the Y Generation. They have grown up with technology; they communicate via their cell phones, Blackberries or laptops. They have had more control over information and communication than any previous generation; they are not unnerved by the pace of change, and are not afraid to question authority. Plainly, they will expect leadership that involves them, motivates them and encourages them to achieve their full potential.

While in this book you will find examples of leaders who are already creative in their various styles and contexts, the real motivation for writing has been twofold. The first is to encourage all teachers to recognise the leadership aspect of their role. The second is to provide both an opportunity for reflection and practical strategies to enable teachers to develop their creative leadership capacity. The underlying theme is really – given our innate potential for creativity, given that the challenges and complexity of our modern world demand more creative approaches – why do we not see more evidence of creativity in educational leadership? As Abraham Maslow suggested, the real question isn't 'what fosters creativity', but rather 'why in God's name isn't everyone creative?'

There has been a particular reason for structuring the book the way it is. The reason is I believe we need to understand where we are and where we have come from before we can appreciate what's involved in getting where we need to be. As you will see, creative thinking starts with what already exists. It's not that we should be looking to the past for solutions, rather that we need to understand why we do things the way be do; we need to be challenging assumptions and practices that have their source in very different times.

So the first part of this book is a series of challenges – they ask you to question why we do things the way we do, why there is so much in education that is rooted in the past. The chapters in Part 1 direct a lens at our modern world in general, and our education system in particular, to examine the barriers that may exist to prevail against creative approaches. The cultural elements that influence how we think about work, about our profession, and about education, may create invisible tensions that direct our behaviour in particular ways. Being aware of the tensions is the first step towards managing them, and freeing ourselves to develop personally and professionally.

Working in education of course, we will experience particular cultural influences exerted by a school, college, district government system. State systems of education have grown to become monolithic entities, and, as in the example of the UK, have increasingly indulged in micro-management strategies in attempting to improve outcomes. Systems thinking also tells us that systems, by their nature, exert immense power to maintain themselves; power that can resist even the most vibrant policy initiatives and energetic individual enterprise. So I don't think I'm alone in believing that, despite individual effort, state systems of education can serve to stifle creative capacity rather than nurture it.

Part II then considers potential solutions to meet the growing demands that a complex world exerts upon education. You won't find a definitive model of creative educational leadership here however. 'One size fits all' does not fit with the notion of creativity itself, nor would it be able to accommodate the many variables in educational contexts. But there are key factors that have been derived from the work and attitudes of the creative leaders interviewed for the purposes of this book. There are also some practical strategies that you may want to draw on to develop personally, professionally and with your relationships.

For most books, the introduction is just that – a brief overview of what follows. Something that perhaps you skip through, or perhaps even ignore completely, preferring to get straight to the main text.

However I'd like to suggest you start thinking now about what you want from this book, and how you want to use it to enhance your personal and professional development. There may be a particular reason why you are choosing to read this book at this particular time: you may want to further your knowledge for some academic endeavour; you may want to learn something to enhance your professional development; you may want to gain an understanding of how to develop your people leadership skills. You may merely be intrigued about how creativity fits with leadership.

This book has been written for all teachers, because all teachers are leaders in their communities and in our society. So whatever your aim, I hope you will find something in this book that you can use to develop your creativity in leadership.

Notes

1 Anna Craft 2005:5
2 Rodney Ogawa and Steven Bossert 1997:9

PART 1

Tensions and challenges

1

The changing nature of learning for work

The speed of technological advances and social changes may feel like the only constant in our lives is change. So this chapter asks you to consider how well you balance *change* with *stability* in your work of preparing young people for their future. You may not find an easy answer; if there was, as Michael Fullan suggests, we would have found it long ago, and there wouldn't be a billion-dollar industry devoted to its pursuit. Even so, 'nothing is more important in the twenty-first century than learning to manage change'.[1]

Television adverts can be irritating when they interfere with the flow of a programme. At other times they are entertainment in themselves. And for the social scientist, they can document the changing nature of life and work in the twenty-first century.

You may have seen a series of advertisements for the Kwik Fit tyre company.

Each advertisement featured a mini scenario. We first see a mechanic describing the service the company can provide to a customer. The customer looks interested, says that's great and then asks 'What else can you do?'. This is the prompt for the mechanic to demonstrate the 'added value'. It's the 'reframe', as in a joke where it's the unexpected that makes us laugh. In one version the mechanic opens a tool-box to reveal a piano that he plays skilfully to the delight of the customer. In another the mechanic clicks his fingers and sends a badly-behaved small boy into a trance to the relief of his hard-pressed mother.

These advertisements are not just creating 'unique selling points' for a tyre fitting company – they capture very neatly the difference in working practices in the twenty-first century compared with the previous industrial era. There's now less clear definition around what 'work' entails. If you call a plumber he will turn up on your doorstep with a laptop rather than a toolbox. If you're considering the purchase of a car, the salesperson is likely to draw on sophisticated techniques that originate in a psychological model such as neuro-linguistic programming. And tyre fitters have to be alert to customer relations. As Daniel Goleman describes it, the rules for work are changing:

'We're being judged by a new yardstick: not just by how smart we are, or by our training and expertise, but also by how well we handle ourselves and each other'.[2]

Change in the organisation of work

We can't escape the fact that the increased competitiveness of the globalisation of economic activity has impacted on how we work at an individual level. Even before the effects of worldwide recession bit into employment, Charles Handy had put down a marker on where the world of work was heading:

'Price wars and quality wars are forcing companies to slim down their employment rolls to a hard core of operatives whose only function is to serve the needs of customers and the tight little nuclei of managers whose only function is to find and hold on to those customers'.[3]

We also can't ignore how the changes in the wider world are impacting upon how young people learn for work. In a highly competitive workplace Richard Gerver[4] estimates that when children starting school now reach retirement age they will have worked in 18-25 different organisations and companies, compared to the four or five companies worked in by those retiring now. Research in the US has estimated that a typical member of Generation Y, current young professionals, will have 10 jobs by the age of 38.[5] And the rapid pace of change is also affecting how businesses operate. Companies will no longer have the expectation that they will train people who will then stick with the business for life. They will employ more and more people on short-term contracts, helping the company with key areas of new development and then moving on as a company's plans and needs change.

Different work for different times

'Conventional structures of work are changing at a rapid rate. More people are working in small organisations, on part-time or fixed term contracts, or on a self-employed basis. Long-term trends identified by the Confederation of British Industry and the Institute of Employment Studies indicate that an increasing proportion of the workforce, currently almost one in four, will become part-time or temporary workers. New and more flexible styles of working will bring with them different or additional demands for learning opportunities for self-management, work and business planning as these groups of workers become increasingly common. More people will work from home and will need to learn how to manage their own activities or to plan their own business'.

Helena Kennedy QC 1998:165

Plainly educational professionals can't stay aloof and separate from changes in the workplace generally. As the globalisation of economic activity has brought increased competitiveness for markets, nation states have been driven to raise the levels of educational achievement of their potential labour forces.[6] The national drive and the need to accommodate additional learning needs have impacted directly upon the work of teachers. They no longer experience their work constrained within the isolation of the classroom. Local groups such as the Education Business Alliance act as brokers between schools, business and community groups: both introducing students to the world of work, and arranging professional development opportunities for teachers with local businesses. Within schools, there's a new emphasis on teachers as leaders of learning, working in teams that may include classroom assistants, learning coaches, mentors.

'This is one of my strengths – I love change, I thrive on change. But I'm also good at empathising with people who don't like change. I want staff to feel comfortable and confident about change. I don't believe in an approach

> *that scares people: I reassure when I can, and always, always call out the benefits – there are always benefits in change, if you want it to be a positive experience'.*
>
> Maria is a Faculty Manager in a Further Education College.
>
> *'Most change in education is externally imposed. Leaders have to be comfortable with change as a feature of the landscape. What matters more is how other people like it – do they want to hide in a cupboard and avoid it. What worries me most is that modern teachers are not trained or prepared to propose their own changes. There's a culture of teacher education designed around delivery of a curriculum rather than promoting the potential for creativity'.*
>
> Richard is a Primary School Headteacher.

As you'll see in the next chapter, people exhibit their own responses to the fluidity of the workplace. In relation to teaching, there's a call to redefine 'part-time' in an age when no person can be guaranteed a job for life. In England, the Teach First initiative placed new graduates in challenging schools, and the young professionals who have been involved suggest ways that collaboration could make teaching a more exciting notion. The development of a Flexible Teacher role would enable teachers to work part of their time in a school and the rest of the time in a dual profession, to the mutual advantage of both:

> '...the Flexible Teacher would develop new skills in a different environment and enjoy a more varied career; schools would be able to retain more excellent teachers, and benefit from the skills and knowledge transfer that the Flexible Teacher would facilitate; the dual profession employer would access the leadership and soft skills of a Flexible Teacher, and pupils would benefit from continued contact with experienced, passionate and multi-skilled teachers, with current experience in workplaces in which pupils might be interested'.[7]

(I had to smile when I read that last passage. Because that was exactly what I did when I first started teaching: I taught half the week in a school and worked the other half as a Research Assistant in a School of Nursing Studies in a University. At that time it wasn't a direct choice, I just took up the job opportunities as they arose. There was certainly no formalised role of a Flexible Teacher. But just like the writers above are anticipating, it had significant advantages for my own personal and professional development, and the students I taught benefited from the wider professional knowledge I could contribute to their learning.)

A change in learning for work

Learning for work, then, is now a very different matter than in the previous industrial age when work was more likely to be manual rather than mental, and individuals were constrained within the narrow requirements of factory production. Despite a more precarious and fluid employment situation, Richard Reeves reckons the change has its advantages:

> 'We are now workers by brain, not hand. Work has become more intellec-
> tually stretching and demanding for more people. It's great news. Workers
> on factory lines have traditionally had to 'shut down' in order to survive.
> Now we all need to be switched on to survive'.[8]

Plainly, if work is now 'more intellectually stretching and demanding' there are greater expectations on education to prepare young people for work. Writers in Australia have described a shift away from narrow workforce competences to the naming of creative capacity as a key economic driver in 'a global knowledge-based economy'. Specifically, they note that academic debate is suggesting a 'creative' disposition to the workplace would involve flexibility, adaptability, self-management and the cultivation of an 'enterprising self'.[9] Sandra Welshman puts it even more succinctly: she argues that, to have successful work futures, young people are more likely to need 'one good qualification plus edgy know-how'.[10]

Actually, I put it a bit more than that. If young people are facing a world where they will have to train and re-train, and will take up occupations that don't even exist at present, then in order to be that adaptable, they will need to learn how to learn. Richard Reeves claims 'People used to learn and then earn. Now we learn as we earn'.[11] A life of learning is ahead of us all, and young people will need to be prepared for that.

CREATIVE LEADERSHIP THINKING SPACE

- What is your personal response to change imposed externally?
- Do you resent it?
- Does it generate stress?
- Are you inclined to challenge it?
- Do you accept it and encourage others to work with it?

New skills for old?

Increased flexibility is only one example of change in the way we work. Technology has changed communication for all of us in both capacity and speed: we can now communicate faster, and with more people than at any other time in history. We can track the growth of that speed and capacity over just a few short years. It has transformed the field of politics: with an e-mail list of 14 million, President Barack Obama was able to directly communicate his campaign messages to an unprecedented number of voters. In the UK, when John Prescott was a Member of Parliament he thought Twitter had become a revelation. In the past, if he needed to get a message out he'd have to convince a paper to publish it; now he could tweet his thoughts.[12] The speed of the transition to 'twittering' has indeed been spectacular: by May 2011 Lady Gaga became the first to crash the barrier to 10 million followers – even more than Barack Obama.

And of course the communication capacity is two-way. In 2009, Daniel Hannan, a backbench MEP, made a three-minute speech in the European Parliament thinking it had been ignored by the media, despite his giving advance notice. Yet when he awoke next morning, his phone was clogged with texts, his email box with messages, and overnight the YouTube clip of his remarks attracted of 36,000 hits.[13]

By the early months of 2011 evidence of the power of electronic means of communication had moved from the personal to the public. During the 'Arab Spring', news of the overthrow of government in Tunisia was the trigger that sent thousands of people in neighbouring states surging onto the streets with similar complaints about their own governments, seemingly without organization other than the 'spreading of the word' via social networking sites. In the UK in August 2011, rioting following the shooting of an individual in London quickly spread to organised looting in the cities of Manchester, Birmingham and Bristol: the initial flame fanned to an incendiary by means of Blackberry messaging.

So now we can blog, post and tweet to whom we like, when we like, and the increased speed and capacity of communication channels has itself created change: it has shifted the balance of power. We are no longer reliant upon politicians and governments controlling the flow of information with press releases and drip-feeding the messages they want us to receive. Individually we can respond directly to what is being said, whoever may be saying it: we can pose questions, we can challenge. Socially, we can organise resistance, whether for good or evil causes. With so much information freely available, part of the 'edgy know-how' that young people need will be the ability to make judgements on the source and credibility of information. The knowledge society has brought a need for an extension of skills: the ability to assess, handle and use a vast amount of information.

The speed of communicating electronically has also impacted on the way we use language: the onset of texting, with language changing before our very eyes, also flags up concerns about standards of literacy. Yet Adrian Elliott argues that the definition of literacy has changed so much over the past 50 years that comparisons over time are largely meaningless. His example that a trusted measure of 1950s literacy was simply for National Service recruits to be able to read a military instruction and write down their personal details, is an indicator of how benchmarks in the past were minimal.[14] But recognizing that there are differing requirements in the twenty-first century is simply not enough. In the UK, although estimates vary, it does appear that by the end of their eleven years compulsory schooling, over 20 per cent of young people still struggle with the basics of the three Rs, with almost 350,000 teenagers a year failing to master the basics of English and Maths.[15] And of course, in addition to 'functional' literacy and numeracy being at a much higher level, there is also a greater need for young people to develop more sophisticated levels of communication and 'soft' skills.

But that's one area where increased use of technological means of communication may not be of benefit. Young people are more likely to keep in touch by text and conduct 'virtual relationships' via social networking sites, leading to a concern that technology has hindered the development of inter-personal skills. The claim from business and industry that graduates arrive with insufficient level of communication and 'soft' skills raises the question of when and how young people will acquire the skills deemed essential for the workplace.

Changing social relationships

We are social animals and through evolution we are designed to live and work socially. Since social relationships are complex and require maintenance by means of an intricate set of interpersonal skills, it may rightly be a source of concern that young people are losing the skills of social interaction due to a dependence upon technology. After all, language is only one channel of communication, and in text and e-mail we miss out on the body language factors that give us a fuller insight into another person's meaning and intention.

Of course we can't lay all of the blame on a preference for communicating electronically rather than personally. The rapid pace of change also applies to society in general. Young people now have less access to family and community groups where in the past they would have had the opportunity to develop and practice interpersonal skills. Those of us of a certain age may indulge in 'neighbourhood nostalgia' and worry about the apparent loosening of community and family ties. But Richard Reeves suggests we can take a different perspective. He claims that community is not dead. The whole basis of social relations has shifted, and new forms of community are being constructed under our noses. Rather than being based around communities, neighbourhoods and friendship groups, 'work has become the central crucible of social relations'.[16]

During their working life, since they are likely to be part of a global workforce, young people will meet up with a wider range of people than any previous generation. But since they are starting from a point where there is less opportunity to learn the basics if community and family ties have weakened, and where technology strips away the nuances of communication, opportunities to prepare for the sophisticated level of interpersonal skills required for a global workplace would seem to be limited. If work is now 'sociable' as well as technical, learning for work will have to take account of that.

CREATIVE LEADERSHIP THINKING SPACE

- In what ways have you been creative in incorporating change into ways of working for yourself and others?

- How active are you in initiating positive changes . . .

. . .to improve the way you work?
. . .to improve the way your team works together?
. . .to improve outcomes for young people?
. . .to instil a positive culture in your organisation?

And what about stability?

John MacBeath writes that the drive for novelty is always in tension with the comfort of the familiar.[17] Indeed, as a counter to what seems to be universal change, some seek stability in the customs, practice and values more commonly exhibited in the past. Head of Mossbourne community academy, Sir Michael Wilshaw, established an educational philosophy that relied upon rigid discipline and traditional approaches to teaching and learning. The policy on uniform is rigidly adhered to, students are sent home if they wear the wrong shoes, hair must be the right length and ties need to be straight. No visits to nearby fast food shops are allowed, even on the way home. There are no mixed-ability classes, students are taught in strictly defined subject areas rather than through the medium of themes, and there's plenty of homework. The authoritarian ethos wouldn't suit everyone, but Wilshaw makes no apologies for the traditional approach, 'A lot of our children come from unstructured, chaotic backgrounds; we need to build more structure into their lives, not less'. It's also an approach that is allowing pupils to achieve success: Mossbourne is expected to be amongst the top three dozen comprehensives in England to have 85 per cent of pupils gaining 5 or more GCSEs at A*-C. This despite being based in Hackney, one of London's more deprived boroughs with 40 per cent of pupils with free school meals, 30 per cent on the special needs register and 80 per cent from ethnic minorities.[18]

The Mossbourne style and philosophy may appear dated and old-fashioned and not find favour with everyone. Yet it is a style that is also reflective of John Carver's view – that commitment to excellence produces change that is more creative than reactive.[19]

CREATIVE LEADERSHIP THINKING SPACE

How does your organisation achieve a balance between a focus on the attainment of qualifications and developing the personal skills, adaptability and well-being of young people?

Anthony is a lecturer at a Further Education college who leads on positive behaviour management for his faculty. He admits there's a tension in balancing the different needs. His focus is on the students, but he also acknowledges the importance of setting boundaries, before they make their own. The college systems for attendance, student goals and recording achievements may be time-consuming, but they establish a clear and stable structure which saves time in the long run. Alongside the formalities, Anthony's approach with the students is flexible: 'I do everything on relationships in the first six weeks, set it up for the year'. For the rest of their course, Anthony has to be creative in order to maintain the ethos he's established: 'Sometimes the groups are so big you don't get the same relationships. So you have to figure out how to work with students as a small team'. Year on year, Anthony's students have maintained consistently high levels of attainment. Yet the experience of the *process* of their learning means they also acquire the skills of working with others alongside their qualification.

It's not just the customs of the more recent past that are put to use to maintain stability in the face of social change. In his research on social groupings, anthropologist Robin Dunbar[20] has included studies of groups of different primates, hunter-gatherer groupings, divisions in the Roman army, Neolithic villages from around 6000 BC and English villages recorded in the Doomsday Book of 1086. A very broad range of samples, from which there appears to be common factor: the size of groups has consistently been around the number 150. Any larger, and groups split to form further groups.

As to whether 150 can be applied in more technologically developed societies, he suggests that once you start to look for them, groups about this size turn up everywhere. He points to the example of modern armies – certainly a sector that is dependent upon the cohesiveness of groups for their effectiveness. And here, the smallest independent unit is a company, made up of three platoons of 30 to 40 soldiers each, which, when you add in command and support staff makes a total of 130–150. There's also the claim from organisational theory that businesses with fewer than 150 people work fine on a person-to-person basis, but any larger and they need a formal hierarchy to work efficiently:

'Sociologists have known since the 1950s that there is a critical threshold in the region of 150 to 200, with larger companies suffering a disproportionate amount of absenteeism and sickness'.[21]

So in relation to group size, big is not necessarily better. Which has a relevance when we think about the shift in organizations to bigger and bigger groupings. Big businesses and big schools may maximise the benefits of economies of scale, but are not necessarily as satisfying for the individuals involved in them. The ones that are really successful arrange their organizations in networks of smaller groupings that retain a local 'intimacy', while still being aligned to the overall mission and values of the 'parent' organisation. As Charles Handy has put it:

'We want villages, even in the midst of our cities. It is no different in organizations. Small may not always be beautiful but it is more comfortable. It is also more flexible and more likely to be innovative'.[22]

But the aspect of interest to us here is how we relate this to learning for work. First, it seems that throughout history the stability of both ape and human groupings has been maintained by keeping groups within a maximum of 150. Secondly, the fact that this still appears relevant for the workplace could stem from Robin Dunbar's hypothesis that it's something about the *quality* of the relationships that is important, not just the absolute number. There appears to be a relationship between the fact that both primates and humans have evolved the biggest brains, and that we are able to maintain complex social relationships. The relative size of the neocortex in particular – the 'new' outer layer of our brain that is mainly responsible for conscious thinking – enables us to maintain social relationships that are immensely complex – but only so far. That's why Robin Dunbar questions the exaggerated claims of having hundreds or thousands of 'friends' on a social networking site. In 'real' relationships, it's not just a matter of remembering who is who, or how they relate to each other and to ourselves, but how we can use that information to manage relationships effectively. And there seems to be a limit to our ability to be able to do this:

> 'The number of people we know personally, whom we can trust, whom we feel some emotional affinity for, is no more than 150, Dunbar's Number. It has been 150 for as long as we have been a species. And it is 150 because our minds lack the capacity to make it any larger'.[23]

The balancing act: Change vs stability

The focus of this chapter has been on learning for work, yet it's also plain that the change and complexity in our modern world has meant there is less definition and separation between the knowledge and skills young people will need for work, and those that will allow them to develop personally and socially. The pace of social and economic changes mean that young people will not just need the qualifications required by the workplace, but need the personal and social skills, the 'edgy know-how' that will enable them to learn as they earn, train and retrain. But finding a balance between qualification needs and personal development needs is not the only challenge for leaders in education. Teachers themselves may feel uncomfortable with the fast pace of change, may cling to familiar ways of working, interpret the changing needs as being expected to 'compensate for society'. It's not a balancing act that can be ignored, and creative leaders find ways of resolving it.

CREATIVE LEADERSHIP THINKING SPACE

- How flexible is your organisation in creating different working experiences for staff and students?

- What do you need to do...

...to be creative in managing change?
...to improve the way you deal with complexity and challenge?
...to improve the flexibility and responsiveness of your organisation?

Notes

1 Michael Fullan 2008:viii–ix
2 Daniel Goleman 1998:3
3 Charles Handy 1995:23
4 Richard Gerver 2010:6
5 'They don't live for work...they work to live'. Anushka Asthana, *The Observer*, 25 May 2008
6 Bob Jeffrey & Anna Craft 2001
7 Alex Kelly & Jen Hall 2009:24
8 Richard Reeves 2001:50
9 Erica McWilliam & Sandra Haukka 2008:655–6
10 Sandra Welshman 2006:50
11 Richard Reeves 2001:51
12 Reported by *The Guardian*, 21st August, 2010
13 Reported in *The Telegraph*, 26 March 2009
14 Adrian Elliott 2007:39
15 Guy Claxton 2008:17
16 Richard Reeves 2001:118
17 John MacBeath 2009:13
18 'Is Mossbourne academy's success down to its traditionalist headteacher?' Peter Wilby, *The Guardian*, 5 January 2010
19 John Carver 1997:211
20 Robin Dunbar 2010:21–34
21 *Ibid.*, p.26
22 Charles Handy 1995:36
23 Robin Dunbar 2010:4

2

Work: Who we are or what we do?

Work is not something that merely fills our time: there is a relationship between our work and how we experience ourselves as individuals. As a creative leader, your approach to your work will influence your colleagues, and also young people. So this chapter asks you to question where you stand in relation to your work as *professionalism*, or as *task-orientation*.

If you think work is just a job we do, and there's no connection to our emotions or who we are, try watching *Masterchef*.

Masterchef is a successful television series that presents contestants with cooking challenges that test their skills, creativity and stamina to the utmost. Contestants are as diverse a group as you can imagine; the common factor is their passion for cooking, together with a desire to become a professional chef.

Since competing becomes an experience that stretches them physically, creatively and emotionally, it's perhaps not surprising that there's a frequent display of emotion when contestants earn the right to progress to the next stage.

Like 2009 winner James Nathan. It's no wonder James shed tears as he was announced the winner. James had harboured a love of cooking since childhood, but trained as a barrister to please his father. A legal career brought no professional satisfaction, and personally, he knew from his first tutorial that he didn't fit in.[1] So he gave up everything, lived on credit for two years, and entered the Masterchef contest to further his ambition to become a renowned chef.

Work, for James, is much more than what he does, it defines him as a person. There is an emotional connection to cooking as work that is his way of expressing his identity, almost as important to him as a physical life-sustaining function. His experience echoes Richard Reeves' view that our work is the principal character in our story of ourselves.[2]

CREATIVE LEADERSHIP THINKING SPACE

Can you recognise an emotional attachment to work for yourself and the people you lead?

Work as our identity

Richard Reeves[3] writes that artists have always seen their work as an expression of themselves, and society has accepted this more readily for them than for other sorts of worker. We can look at a sculpture or a painting – or even a plate of food – and view it as a work of self-expression; it's harder for us to see a new spreadsheet in the same light. But for Richard they are essentially the same. They are both expressions of our abilities, interests and imagination.

> 'For me personally, teaching is not merely something that I 'do' – it is who I am, and defines much of what I say, do and believe.'
>
> Mal Davies, Headteacher (2009)

Richard also makes the point that the link between work and identity is no longer made through the Y chromosome. Women, who make up half the workforce in both the UK and the US, now define themselves in terms of their work rather than their status as wives or mothers:

'Indeed, for women who are in the first generation to enjoy similar opportunities to men at work, the issue of identity is more important than for many of their male peers. The independence that work brings them is hard-won – and therefore hugely significant.[4]

Which reminds me of research I did some years ago investigating the work of mental health nurses. At the time, there was a new government initiative to place nurses at police stations and magistrates courts, to identify people with mental health issues and direct them to appropriate health services. For the nurses, it meant moving from their hospital base to a different working environment; it meant being a single health professional relating to lawyers, police officers, probation officers and magistrates. There was the added dimension that the nurses were mainly female, and the venues of the criminal justice system were – at that time – predominantly male.

All the nurses were very well qualified and experienced in their own profession. Yet working outside their own professional comfort zone, they found it disconcerting to have their professional knowledge questioned, and their recommendations challenged in the cut and thrust of lawyers' adversarial court dialogue. So unsettling in fact, that it struck right to the heart of their feelings about themselves and their professional ability. As one said:

> 'It needed questioning, you know "Are you as good as you are…God, you're doing all this and you sound as if you know what you're doing, but do you really?".'…I'd stopped being a nurse and become something else'. [5]

For this worker, and also for Mal, the headteacher, and James the chef, their work is not something they *do*, it's something they *are*. For the nurse, the challenge to her professional ability was also a threat to her identity – her professional development was so closely linked with her personal development that she experienced them as inseparable. As Richard Reeves writes:

> 'How we work, who we work with and what we work on speaks everlouder volumes about who we are and what we stand for.'[6]

'Good Work'

Howard Gardner and his colleagues have suggested that 'What constitutes good work?' is a question all of us must ask again and again. Specifically, the question is about how we can live up to the demands of our job and the expectations of society without denying the need of our personal identities.[7]

As long ago as the early 1960's philosopher John MacMurray was flagging up the importance of the link between our work and our personal development. He described how as human beings we enter into two basic kinds of relationship with each other: the functional (which has a purpose such as our work) and the personal (which has no purpose other than to enable us to be ourselves). Both are necessary, but the most important point is that the personal is the more important of the two – 'the economic is for the sake of the personal'.[8]

In fact, many find that personal element without any financial reward. Public sector services are supported by thousands and thousands of people who work unpaid – as school and college governors, learning helpers, magistrates; for victim support schemes, physical and mental health charities, hospital audit teams, community health councils, voluntary organisations; in charity shops. Some who only equate work to the value of the pay cheque at the end of the month may question why they do this. But this army of volunteers are made up of people who have discovered that work has other benefits. As you saw in the previous chapter, work is where we develop intellectually, and personally as well. Work is a valid source of social relationships, rather than the virtual relationships of social networking sites. Work can bring a feeling of self-worth, and give meaning to our lives. So when, for whatever reason, paid employment is not available, many people seek out work for themselves.

'Meaningful' work

Phil had worked for a multinational company for 20 years and had always planned to retire at 60. But a sudden and drastic change in company policy that ended its pension plan meant Phil was forced to retire two years earlier. Philosophically, Phil could acknowledge the global changes that were affecting the company: the business world was moving to relying on contract staff rather than permanent employees. It's just that his company was being more ruthless than most. Even so, there was still a niggling resentment that employees once regarded as assets had now become liabilities.

At least the large company he worked for had the capacity to lay on activities to prepare people for the end of their working life. Which, in itself, was a recognition that the end of work is a life-changing event that needs constructive support. On offer was independent advice on how to handle their money, and suggestions on what to do with their time.

As Phil had enjoyed high earnings during his working life he had no need to seek paid employment. But nevertheless, if there was a fear for Phil, it was that he would feel under-utilized. He now had time to keep in touch with extended family and friends but he felt that wouldn't be enough. He already had a role as a governor in his local school, and before very long he was appointed to a local health board. As he sought them out, opportunities began to emerge, and he could even foresee a time when he would have to be selective with his activities.

Phil is one of the lucky ones. For some, a sudden end to paid employment brings economic and social predicaments and can result in psychological trauma. For others, the end of work with nothing to fill the gap can bring feelings of inadequacy and loneliness. For Phil, even though he didn't need to replace his paid employment, he still needed activity – 'work' – to be meaningful, purposeful, to 'feel he was making a difference'. It's not just the economic that's for the personal; whatever our 'work' is, it defines us as individuals and gives our lives meaning.

Unfortunately – as you also saw in Chapter 1 – employment is not the stable, secure environment it was in the past; the changing nature of work means many people are losing their work. Phil was one of the more fortunate ones; he made the transition from paid employment to take a role on public bodies that utilized his skills and gave him personal satisfaction. For others, if there's nothing to replace it, being without work can be experienced as a loss of status, of identity, even of meaning to life. After all, for those of us fortunate enough to work in education, we don't just work as professionals, we are more likely to think of ourselves as *being* a professional person.

Work as professionalism

Andrew Pollard has described the essence of professionalism as 'the exercise of skills, knowledge and judgement for the public good'.[9] On the face of it we are fortunate in having an identity as a 'professional'. However, as the world changes, so does the meaning of words. And the meaning of what it is to be 'professional' has shifted to the degree that almost defies a common understanding.

A hundred years ago, to be a professional meant to have status in society, not only from having ownership of a unique body of knowledge, but also carrying a moral authority that was recognized and given due deference. But as Judith Sachs[10] has pointed out, when we have estate agents referring to themselves as professionals, window-cleaners claiming to provide a professional service and sellers of used cars celebrating a professional code of practice, it's little wonder the meaning of the term has changed, if not been eroded.

Traditionally, professionalism was linked to a particular level of education, as with doctors and lawyers. And associated with qualifications came the moral authority related to the expectation of a certain standard of behaviour. So professionalism was associated with both education AND behaviour. Now they have become separated, and the expectation of 'professionalism' is linked more overtly to standards of behaviour.

Teaching as a profession has never achieved the professional standing of medicine or law, and political and social changes in the recent past now create a question over whether that status would ever be achieved. Mandy Swann and her colleagues[11] suggest that reforms, policy changes and shifts of emphasis over the past 25 years have derailed the traditional aspiration of teachers to have a professionalism similar to that of doctors and lawyers. On the other hand, Harry Cayton's view (see below) is that this traditional idea of professionalism is no longer relevant in our modern world. Indeed, perhaps this traditional view is too elitist and hierarchical to sit comfortably in our more democratic culture. 'Teacher knows best' for instance, may no longer apply in an environment where teachers' practice is shifting them from the 'sage on the stage' to the 'guide on the side'.

Changing professionalism in healthcare

Harry Cayton[12] (2004) is Chief Executive of the Council for Healthcare Regulatory Excellence and as such is concerned with the professionalism of medics and healthcare workers. For Harry, there is a disturbing smugness and self-satisfaction about the traditional definition professionalism, and he questions whether the traditional factors are still relevant in our modern world.

Take **Altruism**: Harry is unsure about whether this is still a significant professional marker. For instance, we wouldn't particularly think of law or accountancy as altruistic professions. While many people in healthcare may be motivated by altruism, such motivation is not necessary to their practice. In fact, the claim of altruism allows the medical profession to claim moral superiority: and it's this certainty of 'goodness' that leads to complacency and worse. Even perhaps in the case of the late Dr Shipman, where the certainty of shared medical goodness, rather than laziness or incompetence, led his colleagues to ignore the evidence before their eyes.

Secondly, Harry finds **mastery** to be an archaic concept. It stems from the Guilds of the Middle Ages, whose members claimed possession of secret knowledge that was with-held from others. Nowadays, while a body of knowledge is still essential, equally it is the *interpretation* of knowledge, the *engagement* with new knowledge and the *sharing* of knowledge which are also characteristics of modern medicine.

Thirdly, Harry mentions **autonomy** as the expectation of a professional, and concludes that professional autonomy is already gone. As he puts it:

'...I think the medical profession is finding that the most painful loss of all. It's gone because of the very complexity of applying knowledge; people can't do it well if they try to do it alone. It's going because of standards, guidelines, re-validation, regulation, contracts, decision-support and team-work.'

So having found the traditional definition of professionalism to be out-dated and irrelevant, Harry offers alternative characteristics as a way of generating self-respect and pride in doing medicine. He suggests:

Empathy: Concentration on the individual other, communicating, working in partnership, with consent, courtesy, respect, supported self-management and choice

Expertise: Applying knowledge rather than mastery of a body of knowledge.

Mutuality: Rather than autonomy; defining a new professionalism in terms of relationships:

- with knowledge
- with colleagues
- with patients
- with society

And in addition, Relationship with self: demonstrated by reflection and self-knowledge, and the ability to judge how the other relationships are working.

You may find that Harry's analysis resonates with the way the profession of teaching is changing. There has been much written about the need for the profession to match our more open and knowledgeable society by moving our practice from 'teacher' to 'facilitator'.[13] Young people of the twenty-first century do not conform to the passive compliant model of classes of the past, and teaching has had to adapt to developing active independent learners to enable them to meet the challenges they will face.

CREATIVE LEADERSHIP THINKING SPACE

What do you think of the analysis of the changing nature of professionalism in the medical profession? Would it also apply to the education sector?

Perhaps Harry's ideas about the more important elements of professionalism have general application. Empathy, for instance, the ability to
communicate and work in partnership; applying knowledge rather than
retaining mastery would certainly seem relevant to a world where knowledge
is doubling every seven years; and a professionalism defined in terms of
relationships, in all its aspects. It's a definition that is also reflected in the
views of existing leaders.

> *'Professionalism is to do with how you conduct yourself during the day, how
> you conduct relationships with others. You have to have mutual respect with
> people you deal with – with the children, with everyone. It's not professional
> to think you're better than anyone else, that the child is less important than
> you'.*
>
> Janet is a Primary School teacher
>
> *'Professionalism of a leader is about having a clear vision that is both
> communicated to staff and engages them. Engaging staff in the overall
> vision for their college means making it explicit at all levels: you have to
> 'walk the talk', be a follower as well as a leader. Professionalism is not
> about qualifications, it's about having clear communication, being open and
> honest'.*
>
> Dick is Principal of a Further Education college
>
> *'Teachers are highly professional as far as standards of teaching etc., but
> deficient in relation to inter-professional working. They don't find it easy
> to mix with other professionals. They must be confident to work across /
> between professions'.*
>
> David is Director of an Institute for Applied Education Research

Work as expert behaviour

Teachers and leaders may make a thousand decisions in a day, and they make
them by drawing both on the knowledge acquired during their training and
that derived from their personal experience. Much of this knowledge will be
'tacit'; although teachers will intuitively know what they know, and leaders
will understand 'what works', they may find it difficult to articulate what they
know.

This doesn't only apply to teachers and leaders of course, but to any expert behaviour. My mother was a very good cook, but unfortunately she was never able to pass on her skill to her daughter because she was unable to give a precise account of how to create a particular dish. And also because she wasn't the soul of patience! I remember asking her how much of an ingredient was needed for a particular cake, and she could only reply 'Oh, you **know**'. Because she of course 'knew' by touch, sight and judgement rather than measurement. Indeed, research on expert behaviour has been consistent in showing that the knowledge base of expert behaviour is tacit and therefore defies easy explanation.

The classic work of Nikolai Bernstein in the early years of the twentieth century illustrated the inadequacy of trying to break down expert behaviours into a list of competences. His analysis of the actions of blacksmiths showed that, although repeated blows of the hammer appeared to be similar, they were in fact produced by an infinitely variable combination of movements of the shoulder, elbow and wrist. Like a blacksmith, a good teacher may repeat the same lesson many times, but the elements of their approach and behaviour will be adjusted each time to suit the circumstances.

We live in complex times, and leadership is complex behaviour. The theory of complexity tells us that complex systems are composed of huge numbers of small elements, and there are multiple feedback loops by which the elements influence each other, but, as David Turner puts it, these are not the most important elements:

'The most important element is that complex systems cannot, in principle, be analysed through breaking them down into the constituent components. The system as a whole, and its sub units, have 'emergent properties' which cannot be understood as merely the sum of the properties of smaller units'.[14]

CREATIVE LEADERSHIP THINKING SPACE

How do you see your leadership as creative in developing people's expert behaviour?

Work as task-orientation

Despite this analysis of complex behaviours, there is a prevailing emphasis that seeks to classify 'expert' work as a series of competences. Bodies such as the Teacher Training Agency in the UK have developed a list of over 100 competences that make up the repertoire of an effective teacher. Yet Bernstein's studies indicate that such a list of competences will not necessarily produce expert performance: the expert practitioner controls the whole action, adjusting the elements in order to create the whole, but not necessarily repeating any element exactly.

The competence approach could be seen as an attempt to rationalise complex behaviour. In fact, there is a view that the whole of society is being influenced in this direction. It's not a new view amongst sociologists, but it's been taken a step further by George Ritzer in his concept of *McDonaldization*[15], where he suggests the workplace as a whole is adapting to the principles of the fast-food restaurant. The principles relate to efficiency, predictability and control, and also calculability – in other words, that the outcome should be quantifiable. It's a view in direct conflict with the idea that our twenty-first century society is complex, multi-faceted, and different from a previous industrial era. But Ritzer claims the principles of McDonaldization are influencing society at an accelerating rate, even impacting upon healthcare and education.

Unfortunately, the competence approach – together with the suggestion that education is being influenced by the McDonaldization of society generally – encourages a view of teaching as task-orientated activity rather than professional expertise. Many have bemoaned this approach as an encroachment upon the professionalism of teachers. For some, delivering someone else's predesigned, scripted and timed packages can be equated to 'teaching by numbers'.[16] Andy Hargreaves[17] even describes it as reducing teachers to karaoke singers, learning only to follow the bouncing ball of the script.

Indeed, the idea of work as task-orientation, as standardized actions as in McDonaldization, is in conflict with a view of work as part of our identity, an activity where we can develop expertise, and which is closely aligned to our personal development. It's also at odds with research findings that the ability to learn from experience may be more important than existing competency levels, particularly in view of the fact that the skills needed tomorrow may not be exactly the same as those needed today.[18] As you will see from the views expressed by John McBeath, it is a challenge that leadership needs to address:

'...teachers are not, or ought not to be simply technicians, implementing or 'delivering' a curriculum. If they are truly to be seen as professionals their focus must be on learning, building their professional knowledge through observation, inquiry, discussion with colleagues, reading theoretical texts and keeping up to date with developments in the field – not just in their subject matter field but with an interest in the art and science of teaching. To effect this we also believe that leadership and critical friendship play a key supportive and challenging role'.[19]

CREATIVE LEADERSHIP THINKING SPACE

- Do you experience yourself as *being* a professional?
- What are the implications of having an expectation of *all* those you lead to act 'professionally'?
- Or is your expectation that people will 'do their jobs'?
- How do you think your expectations are demonstrated – in what you say, in what you do?

Work and young people

Of course if we accept the importance of work to our identity and personal development, we shouldn't neglect applying those arguments to children and young people. For the youngest, it's be easy for us to recognize that play is their work, and to acknowledge the need for play to be creative and to stimulate a child's overall development. We can see this acknowledged in policy developments such as in Wales, with the introduction of a curriculum for 3–7 year olds where learning is constructed around play rather than formal teaching.

But as they grow older – and indeed for us as adults – there's a tendency to no longer view learning as playful, but to categorise it as 'work'. And then of course the experience becomes standardized, formalised, enveloped in an overall culture of 'schooling'. What 'playful' bits of the educational experience there are will tend to be viewed as a release from an overall requirement that young people approach their learning as 'hard work'. But if we accept the link between our work and our personal development, we must also apply this to young people, and recognize that the well-being and sense of identity of young people will be integral to their learning (their work).

Of course, as mentioned previously, there is a movement towards a more creative paradigm in education; a movement away from complete dependence on a model of operant conditioning (moulding young people by means of rewards and punishment). It is a movement that has been stimulated by developing knowledge from neuroscientists about how the brain works, and from constructivist theories relating to the need for learners to be actively engaged in constructing their own meaning. And in addition there is the influence of changes in our social and economic environment that mean young people need to be active engaged learners in order to cope with the fast pace of change of our modern world.

Part of this more creative paradigm has been a movement towards brain-based learning: the engagement in educational practices based on an understanding of how the brain works. Interestingly, Eric Jensen introduces the concept not just as a way of thinking about learning, but also as a way of thinking about our job.[20] Learning about learning is not just about applying a few brain-based techniques; a brain-based school must become a learning organization. And that involves leaders and teachers being aware of the existing culture, establishing a learning climate, building a collective vision. Part of establishing a learning organization is also about how the individuals concerned view their own work: do members have their own personal vision, are they making progress, feeling empowered? In other words, our approach to our own work has an impact on the young people we work with. Work can be what we do – just a job. Or we can experience work as part of our personal development, something that occupies us physically, mentally and emotionally, something that requires a commitment to lifelong learning to get the best of out it. Since leaders and teachers are role models, it follows that the way we model our own work will have a direct impact upon young people. As Eric Jensen says:

'As you model lifelong learning, others will be more likely to follow. If you believe it, live it'.[21]

The balancing act:
Professionalism vs task orientation

This chapter has asked you to consider the relationship of your work to who you are as an individual. How work is viewed has a direct impact on how it is experienced. The fact that so many people seek out unpaid work is an indicator of its importance at a social and emotional level. It therefore follows that work viewed as a series of tasks will not have the same emotional connection as work experienced as 'being' a professional. How we experience our work will also impact upon those we work with, particularly as teachers and leaders in education are role models for young people. Creative leaders in education recognise that how they place their emphasis in relation to professionalism and task orientation will impact, not just on the people they lead, but upon the overall approach to learning for young people within their school or college.

CREATIVE LEADERSHIP THINKING SPACE

• Where do you think the balance lies between *professionalism* and *task orientation* in your leadership?

• What sort of role model do you present in relation to the way you experience your work as a leader?

• What do you need to do...

  ... to be creative in developing your own expertise?
  ... to recognise and nurture expertise in others?
  ... to make work socially and emotionally satisfying for those around you?

Notes

1 *The Sunday Times.* 15 February 2009.
2 Richard Reeves 2001:41
3 *Ibid.* 2001:37
4 *Ibid.* 2001:33
5 This research was first published in Turnbull & Beese 2000, and I've also included an extract in Turnbull 2007:18–19
6 Richard Reeves 2001:38
7 Howard Gardner et al. 2011:34–35
8 John MacMurray 1961:187
9 Andrew Pollard 2009
10 Judith Sachs 2003:1
11 Mandy Swann et al. 2010:552–3
12 Thanks to Harry Cayton for permission to include this account of his ideas.
13 Gudmundsdottir 1990, Pachier et al. 2003, Atkinson 2004, Korthagen 2004, Dragovic 2007, Richard Churches & John West-Burnham 2008, Jacquie Turnbull 2009
14 David Turner 2010:31
15 George Ritzer 2011
16 See Jacquie Turnbull 2007:6–7
17 Andy Hargreaves 2003:58
18 Spreitzer, McCall & Mahoney 1997
19 John MacBeath 2009:74
20 Eric Jensen 2008:4
21 *Ibid.* 2008:247

3

Schooling as a system

This chapter asks you to consider schooling as a 'system' within which there are forces that may often produce unexpected results. In this respect, Time Control and Teacher Autonomy are suggested as influences that may create a tension within the system. As a creative leader, you may need to be alert to how the tension may impact upon educational experiences and outcomes.

I once teased a class by asking them did they think a river could flow upstream. No of course not was the answer; from their world view it was the nature of a river to flow down to the sea. Then I told them about the St John River in New Brunswick, and the phenomenon of the *Reversing Falls*. The river flows into the Bay of Fundy through a narrow gorge running through the centre of the town of Saint John. Every day, the power of the turning tide pushes ocean water up through the gorge and forces the river to reverse its flow for several hours.

Then I might tell them about the nature of a *bore*, and in particular the one that occurs on the Severn Estuary that separates South Wales from the West of England. During the highest tides, the 30 mile estuary becomes a narrow funnel that forces the incoming tide into a wave that travels up the river for nearly 2 ½ hours. The Severn Bore is a unique natural phenomenon that attracts surfers who aim to ride the wave the length of the estuary, and visitors who seek the best viewing spots to watch as the wave speeds upstream.

You might be curious enough to want to know more about exactly how the Bore occurs, and how it is that it can be predicted with such certainty. In which case, in addition to the unique physical arrangement of the estuary, you would need to take account of other elements that come together to influence the whole:

Wind speed and direction
Depth of freshwater
Low or high air pressure
When the new or full moon occurs
Scouring of the estuary

In this case, you would be studying the Severn Bore as a 'system'. You would be looking at the event as a number of elements interacting together, producing an outcome that is the product of the whole, rather than the independent parts. Peter Senge points out that in this respect living systems have integrity; their character depends upon the whole. And he says the same is true for organizations; it's necessary to see the whole system to be able to understand the most challenging managerial issues.[1] The learning from system thinking – as for my class with the examples of the Reversing Falls and the Severn Bore – is never to take anything for granted.

A world of systems

There are some things in life that we become so accustomed to that we don't feel a need to question them. Words can be like that; regular use becomes automatic and means we don't always stop to analyse what they really mean. The word 'system' is applied to so many aspects of life that you probably don't often reflect on it as a concept introduced by Plato, Aristotle and Euclid. We refer to the solar system or the eco-system. We use it in referring to organizations as in education system, criminal justice system, national health system. We label our own bodies as series of systems – nervous, digestive, cardiovascular. And then of course there are technical applications as in central heating system or air-conditioning system.

However, switching to 'systems thinking' may mean changing the habit of a lifetime. In the Western world, our culture and education has conspired towards acceptance of linear thinking as the default perspective. Peter Senge popularised the concept of systems thinking for organisations as the key to coping with ever more complex future. But he also suggested that our abilities as systems thinkers were underdeveloped, or had even been repressed by formal education in linear thinking.[2]

Joseph O'Connor and Ian McDermott also think our habitual way of thinking is insufficient to deal with systems because we tend to see simple sequences of cause and effect that are limited in time and space, rather than a combination of factors that mutually influence each other. And in addition:

> 'In a system, cause and effect may be far apart I time and space. The effect may not be apparent until days, weeks, even years later. And still we have to act now'.[3]

Thus our tendency to think in terms of cause and effect as having a direct and linear relationship can blind us to the potential for unintended consequences; as with the Reversing Falls and the Severn Bore, how the combination of a multiple factors can produce the unexpected.

Adopting 'systems thinking' may also mean breaking out of the traditional mould of 'management' practice, with its language of targets and 'performativity'. It means adopting a more holistic view that takes account of relationships, of the complexity of the dynamics between people and practices that produce unexpected outcomes. It means aiming to release the creative capacity that can be curtailed within boundaries of entrenched attitudes and embedded practices.

The use of the term 'schooling' in this chapter – as opposed to education – has been deliberate. Education for me is the much broader concept that will be debated in the next chapter. Schooling is used to denote the 'system' that delivers state education. Using the term also makes it easier to keep the examination on features of the *context* of education and the assumptions we hold about that context, as we try to understand how – even with the best of intentions – unexpected effects can arise.

CREATIVE LEADERSHIP THINKING SPACE

Does thinking of 'schooling' as a 'system' make you think of your own context any differently? Can you identify features of the wider system that influence your leadership in your own context?

Resistance to change

Obviously the system of schooling overall is made up of numerous sub-systems nesting within it. While this makes it a complex system, it is not necessarily an unstable one. Complex systems maintain *homeostasis*: a dynamic self-regulation that allows the system to maintain itself in the face of disturbances. Overall stability is a very important aspect in enabling organizations to weather minor and routine challenges, but it comes with a price. The price is resistance to change.[4] Despite persistent attempts, the schooling system demonstrates *inertia* in its resistance to reform.

You need look no further than the curriculum to see evidence of resilience. When state education was first introduced, the curriculum was influenced by what universities thought were important subjects. The hierarchical framework gave first importance to Language, Mathematics and Science, followed by the Humanities, with the Arts in third place. Guy Claxton notes 'astonishingly', that this structure seems to have survived wave after wave of educational reform virtually unscathed. The list of subjects in the 1988 National Curriculum was virtually identical to those introduced in the 1904 Secondary School Regulations.[5]

It's not that there has been a lack of political or professional will to stimulate change in order to raise standards. Numerous reforms in the UK have entailed 20 Education Acts over as many years. In addition, prior to the economic recession, there were significant increases in spending on education. Despite this, there was 'almost no acceleration' in the performance of pupils[6], and it still seems to be the case that our system of schooling is failing to achieve the desired outcomes.

In the UK, underachievement rates have stalled, with little change since the mid-1990s in the percentage of young people aged 16–24 without qualifications, averaging 13.2 per cent over the four UK countries.[7] If we benchmark ourselves against other countries, the results of the OECD Programme for International Student Assessment (PISA) show that all the countries in the UK rate very poorly against 57 other countries when testing 15-year-olds in English, Mathematics and Science.

Plainly a lack of basic skills or qualifications affects employment opportunities, and this is not an issue that shows any improvement. In 2005 the percentage of 16 to 24 year-olds classified as unemployed averaged nine per cent. Yet significantly the percentage of those not in education, employment or training (NEETs) was around twice as high.[8] By 2011 the number of NEETs in England hit a record 1.16 million, 119,000 more than the previous year, a rise of 18 per cent.[9] While economic recession has plainly impacted upon youth unemployment, these figures still indicate a devastating number of young people either unwilling or unable to engage in education or training.

Educational underachievement also affects the relative performance of the economy in the UK, where output per hour is between 10 and 25 per cent lower than France, Germany and the US. Much of this can be attributed to a poorer level of skills and a shortfall of capital investment.[10] In financial terms, the productivity loss to the economy as a result of youth unemployment is estimated at £10 million every day.[11]

There is also a strong relationship between educational underachievement and crime. But perhaps the saddest indicator comes from the 2007 UNICEF report *An overview of child well-being in rich countries*. Educational well-being was one of the six dimensions used in comparing the 21 countries in the report. When it came to ranking, the UK and the US are in the bottom third for five of the six dimensions, with the UK bottom of the twenty-one countries overall.[12] So it appears our young people are not only underachieving educationally, they are unhappy as well.

From a systems perspective all these indicators clearly demonstrate that no system operates in isolation. Inertia in our system of schooling does not only impact upon level of educational achievement, it impacts upon the economic system of our country, the criminal justice system, upon systems of health and welfare.

There have been plenty of attempts to prize inertia out of the school system in order to raise standards and improve outcomes. For people working in the system it may feel that change has been the only constant factor. Government intervention has gradually moved through the school gates to impact upon not just 'what' to teach, but 'how' to teach it. Indeed, it's not that government attempts to micro-manage have been without success. Michael Fullan cites the effect of the National Literacy and Numeracy Strategies in England as a remarkable achievement: some 20,000 primary schools moved forward on average from 62 per cent proficiency in literacy for 11-year-olds in 1997 to 75 per cent in 2000, with similar results being obtained in numeracy. However, there are two related problems with the initiative. First, the results have plateau'ed since 2000, and secondly, heads and teachers did not have a sense of ownership over the strategies. Michael Fullan suggests this lack of ownership accounts for the inability to go beyond the 75 per cent. It's not that lack of deep ownership is merely a matter of commitment, rather:

'Without engagement you don't get the ingenuity and creativity of practitioners that is necessary for developing new and better solutions'.[13]

It's an example that confirms the claim made by system thinkers that to move beyond the standards plateau to create sustainable change means aligning all parts of the system so that they are engaged and moving in the same direction.

CREATIVE LEADERSHIP THINKING SPACE

Can you think of other examples from your experience that indicate a process of *inertia* is preventing system shifts?

'Tinkering' with the structure

Politicians of course want quick fixes. Their sights are on the next election, and they want strategies that demonstrate improvements to voters in the short term. But one of the reasons the Literacy and Numeracy strategies did not bring sustainable improvement was that government aimed for something that would have the biggest and fastest effect possible on learning. So rather than change the structure of education or improve the quality of teachers, it decided to dictate exactly what teachers did.[14]

> '*In leadership, you need political judgement, being able to weigh up what they could do. Defense against political surprises is an important survival strategy'.*
>
> Richard – Primary School Head

Of course more radical reform is a long-term and expensive process, and thus not very seductive politically: which is perhaps one of the reasons why the structure of the system of schooling has proved remarkably resistant to change. In addition to maintaining the same basis for the curriculum, our system of schooling is organised around a structure designed to meet the needs of the nineteenth and twentieth centuries. Both the structure and practice of schooling is so embedded that we hardly question whether this is the way things should be done. As Guy Claxton says, it is as if we hold the basic institution of school in such reverence that we simply cannot conceive of ever doing more than tinkering with it.[15] Thus there's a 'cultural lag' between the system of schooling and the complex learning needs of the twenty-first century that persists.

Sir Ken Robinson describes how systems of education in Europe and the United States were designed to meet the labour needs of an industrial economy based on manufacturing, steel production, engineering and the related trades. For this, they needed a workforce that was roughly 80 per cent manual and 20 per cent professional and managerial, and this assumption underpinned the whole basis of schooling and higher education. The 1944 Education Act in Britain set up a structure of schooling to serve the needs of industrial society: grammar schools were to educate the 20 per cent who would be the professionals and managers; those educated in secondary modern schools encountered a watered-down version of the grammar school curriculum and were destined for manual work. This was a model adopted by many European countries, and more importantly the underpinning assumptions were consistent with the nature of the wider economy and society:

'The assumption was clear-cut and accepted. If a person worked hard at school and gained good academic qualifications, and especially if they went to university, they were assured of secure, lifelong employment in a professional or office job. For over 100 years this narrative has been true and the system has worked well for those who successfully followed its rules'.[16]

Guy Claxton takes the analogy even further, by suggesting *the school as a factory* is an appropriate representation of today's educational system. As schooling expanded to serve the needs of the Industrial Revolution, the most relevant model of the time was the factory. Thus the organization of school and the design of a factory is no coincidence: even the architecture is similar. Students are sent down the production line in batches arranged by age. Knowledge can be standardized and chopped up into different sized bits to be bolted on the students' mind bit by bit. Quality control is assured by regular testing and grading. Failures are usually attributed to inherent faults such as 'low ability' or 'laziness'. Since the workforce cannot be trusted of itself to be responsible, external forms of quality control are imposed, with teams of inspectors visiting the production line to check everything is carried out as ordered. Although many 'operatives' would see their work in different terms – as gardeners nurturing growing plants for instance, Guy Claxton claims 'the deep embedding of the production line model in every facet of school life continually works against such competing metaphors'.[17]

We do indeed cling to these basic assumptions about schooling, despite the fact that we are no longer in an industrial age, that more and more young people are seeing schooling as irrelevant to their lives, that business complains that young people leave school ill-equipped to meet the complex needs of the twenty-first century workplace. Guy Claxton believes it's plain that, if we have not yet figured out how to educate young people in a way that enables the vast majority to feel they have gained something valuable, then it must indicate a basic fault in the system.[18] Sir Ken Robinson is clear that the system is not responsive to our current needs:

'It is not working any more. The reason is the extraordinary nature of technological and economic change. We are caught up in a new economic revolution. And it has hardly begun. Education and training are meant to be the long-term answer for all of those asking how they are to survive the coming turbulence. But they will not provide the answer while we continue to misunderstand the question that this new revolution is presenting'.[19]

CREATIVE LEADERSHIP THINKING SPACE

What is your view of the analysis of schooling as a system designed for a previous industrialist age?

Understanding how change can be implemented

Plainly there appears to be a need to bring about real change; change that has the capacity to meet the complex learning needs of the twenty-first century, and that will be both sustainable and responsive to changing needs.

The usefulness of systems theory is that it is not merely about reducing things to their simplest form to make them understandable and manageable. That would mean missing out on an understanding of how the whole is different from the sum of its parts. Not better, not worse, but certainly different; responsive in different ways, having a different dynamic. Rather, systems theory suggests that complex systems share certain organising principles regardless of content.[20] An understanding of these principles can not only reveal how unforeseen outcomes occur, but also indicate how the behaviour of the system can be influenced.

One of the main principles is that all systems function on different sorts of *feedback*. For instance, we have already seen how deeply held assumptions about the structure and content of schooling appear to restrict the capacity for change. The inability to shift a mental model of what schooling should be about acts as *balancing* (or negative) *feedback* – so that whenever change is introduced, it acts to dampen the effect and limit growth. In the previous example, the levelling off of results of the National Literacy and Numeracy strategies suggests the lack of ownership by heads and teachers would have acted as *balancing feedback*.

Reinforcing feedback, on the other hand, acts by amplifying change, as with a snowball rolling downhill collecting snow as it rolls, getting larger and larger until it becomes an avalanche. Joseph O'Connor and Ian McDermott point out that it's misleading to think of this as *positive* feedback because it depends what change is being amplified: it may be good, or it could be a disaster:

> 'Reinforcing feedback drives a system in the way it is going. It may lead to growth or decline, depending on the starting conditions. Reward is part of a reinforcing feedback loop if it leads to more of the same behaviour. Reward may be a gift, money, encouragement attention or even a smile. Your action, the reward and your repeated action is the reinforcing feedback loop. Reward by itself is not reinforcing feedback, unless it leads to more of the same.[21]

We've seen that desired change can be met with resistance in a system, however when change does occur, it often happens rapidly and sometimes quite dramatically. The fall of the Berlin Wall in 1989 was a good example, and events in North Africa in 2011 saw the spectacular fall of governments that had been in power for decades. We can recognize in ourselves how sustained pressure can lead to a sudden breakdown; load enough pressure onto individuals and you'll eventually reach a point where even a small incident will prompt them to lose their temper, exhibit road rage, walk out on a job, leave a partner. 'The last straw that broke the camel's back' is often the metaphor that people rely upon on to explain such crises.

These examples illustrate that there is a threshold past which a system can exhibit a sudden breakdown, seemingly out of all proportion to the nature of the incident. The good news is that the reverse is also true. The principle of *leverage* suggests that finding the critical point of intervention can result in positive change for very little effort.

In his best-selling book, Malcolm Gladwell gave a range of real-life examples of 'how little things can make a big difference'. His notion of 'Tipping Points' overturns any idea that the way we communicate and process information is straightforward and transparent. Rather, understanding how little things provide leverage for large-scale change relies on us reframing the way we think about the world. It also requires a bedrock belief that change is possible, and that people can radically transform their behaviour or beliefs in the face of the right kind of impetus:

> 'Tipping Points are a reaffirmation of the potential for change and the power of intelligent action. Look at the world around you. It may seem like an immovable, implacable place. It is not. With the slightest push – in just the right place – it can be tipped'.[22]

Identifying the critical points in a system also means recognising the influence that is preventing the change. We used to joke in school that the most important person in the establishment was not the headteacher, but the caretaker. A 'more than my job's worth' attitude can hinder if not block new initiatives, in the same way that any individual who holds the keys, or manages the finances, can raise issues that stifle enterprise. But winning over this key person, establishing rapport with them, may be more effective that influencing a person higher up the chain of command.

Operating the principle of *leverage* can have more effect for less effort. Finding the small but crucial point of influence can be more effective than exerting sustained and heavy-handed pressure – as long as we keep in mind a key factor, as Joseph O'Connor and Ian McDermott remind us:

> '...do not mistake the leverage point as the cause. We know that we can get a big shift if we change the right element, but that does not mean that element was the cause of the trouble, only that changing it was the easiest way to change the structure of the system because of the knock-on effect'.[23]

CREATIVE LEADERSHIP THINKING SPACE

- Can you recognise how balancing feedback may be hindering your attempts to stimulate change?

- Can you think of an example where reinforcing feedback may be amplifying change for the better – or for the worse?

- Can you identify potential points of leverage? In your own institution? In your local district? At a political level?

Sustainable change

While it may be possible to use systems thinking to recognise and influence change in a system such as in a single school, as we have seen, it hasn't been as easy to effect change to the whole system of schooling. Michael Fullan suggests the reason systems *thinking* has not had radical effects is because we need systems *action*. He suggests a new kind of leadership is necessary for breaking through the status quo since – as we have seen – systemic forces (*inertia*) have the upper hand in preventing system shifts. The key factor is being able to achieve *alignment* of the whole system, so that all parts are moving in the same direction. His proposal for what's needed has been a tri-level reform perspective: addressing school and community, district or local education authority, state or national policy.[24]

Policy makers have been picking up on Michael Fullan's recommendations and putting in place strategies to achieve tri-level reform. In Wales, the layered approach to system leadership raises the expectation that heads at local level will be almost as concerned with the success of neighbouring schools as with their own. The best would be selected to fulfil the role of 'system leaders', sharing practice and principles across districts as a basis for local alignment. At national level, a commitment to the success of every learner is envisaged as providing the focus for system-wide transformation and collaboration.

But alignment to achieve reform is about more than consolidating existing management practices or substituting an additional layer. Traditional management practices in the public sector have appeared incapable of dealing with the complexity associated with dynamic environments.[25] Reform also requires a holistic mindset that can accommodate complexity.

Public sector systems have tended to become increasingly bureaucratic and perhaps the question needs to be posed whether despite its size and complexity, does a system need to be overly *complicated*? Taking an illustration from the retail sector may help towards a different view. As an example of creative leadership, Sir Terry Leahy's is a classic bottom-up success story. From a fairly ordinary upbringing in Liverpool he rose to become head of Britain's largest private sector employer. With a workforce of 350,000 (and another 125,00 worldwide), under his leadership Tesco turned over £1 billion a week and in 2009 made more than £3 billion profit.

Despite his success he remained grounded in the real world, driving himself to work at a modest office on an industrial estate. This down-to earth approach is crucial to the way he approached his business, and is also reflected in his views on education:

'One thing the government could do is simplify the structure of our education system. From my perspective there are too many agencies and bodies, often issuing reams of instructions to teachers, who then get distracted from the task at hand: teaching children'.

'At Tesco we try to keep paperwork to a minimum, instructions simple, structures flat and above all we trust the people on the ground. I'm not saying that retail is like education, merely that my experience tells me that, when it comes to the number of people you have in the back office, less is more'.[26]

There are implications in these words for the challenge being set in this chapter – that is, how to balance Time Control and Autonomy. The balance of these two conflicting issues is relevant to reform of the system, so we need to go back to a more detailed perspective for the moment to examine the impact on the education system, and how these issues may be influencing a failure to achieve large-scale reform.

Working in industrial time

So going back to the issue of schooling operating an industrial model, perhaps where this is most evidently at odds with the complexity of our modern world is in the pervading influence of time organisation. Richard Reeves points out that the nine-to-five concept is so deeply embedded in popular language and culture that it's easy to forget what a recent invention it is. In pre-industrial times, work was centred around the home, it had a more fluid and variable nature, it varied according to the season, the time of the week, the weather, even the mood of the individual. Industrialisation changed all that. For the first time, workers had to leave home to work, and because factories couldn't operate on the basis of people working when they felt like it, industrialists needed to take control of workers' time. The operation of machines required a full complement of workers to be on hand at the same time and all the time. So factory time was bounded and measured, reaching its peak in the Taylorist 'time-and-motion' studies of the early part of the twentieth century.[27]

Schooling operates in 'industrial time'. It proceeds in a linear fashion, with the school day, week, term and year forming a sequence of events. It is designed to contain learning as the work of children and young people within a specific time frame. Yet the rigidity of timetabling sits ill at ease with the development of independent learning, and with maximising the creative capacity of students and workers alike. Schooling in many ways operates 'producer capture' – where a service (or system) is organised around the needs of the organisation, rather than the needs of the customer/consumer/client. Richard Reeves claims that we are simply continuing, blindly, to ape the patterns of industrial working life long after the need for them has passed.

I was reminded of the influencing power of the way we think about time when there was a management vacancy at my school. I asked a colleague whether he was going to apply for it. 'Ooh, no fear', was his response, 'that's a 7.00 to 7.00 job'. And indeed I've heard similar comments subsequently where the nature of a leadership role is referred to as 'time spent'. In the wider world, a less rigid concept of time has been popularised by flexible working hours, working from home and even an Age Discrimination Act that allows people to be gainfully employed past pensionable age. Yet as you'll see from the illustration below, in education time has a dominance that can sometimes result in an inflexible approach to working practice.

Work, time – and mindset

We can become so used to our ways of working that sometimes we can't even conceive of doing anything differently. At a school I worked in some years ago, there was an initiative to introduce elements of a shared timetable with the local further education college. This was in response to directives urging us towards provision of more flexible course provision for sixth-formers. Good in theory, but when you got down to the practicalities of timetabling, the devil was indeed in the detail. The process of negotiation wasn't helped by some of the teachers involved, who appeared unable to conceive of working in any way differently from their established practice. Plainly, it made no sense to have students or staff flitting between the school and the college for individual lessons, so one proposal was that the students would have a whole day on their chosen subject. Yet as a potential solution, this met with strong resistance from one teacher in particular. I remember her telling me that she had given it some thought, but she couldn't *possibly* conceive of teaching the same subject all day.

In those days, I divided my time between teaching, and professional training. And with my professional trainer hat on I wouldn't contemplate running a training course for *less* than a day. Having a stretch of time meant I could create a varied programme of learning activities, I could factor in time for reflection, time to consolidate learning. My colleague on the other hand, was so used to planning her teaching around 45 minute slots, that she couldn't even begin to think of doing it any other way – irrespective of the possibility that a different arrangement might have provided a valuable learning experience for the students.

Professional autonomy

The opposing challenge in relation to the controlled regime of schooling, is professional autonomy. At a practical level, it may seem that the time pressures of the system of schooling serve to constrain the autonomy of learners. But the reforms of schooling in the 1980s had led Lesley Kydd to question whether teachers could any longer define themselves as autonomous professionals:

'. . .can claims to professional autonomy be sustained in a situation where the curriculum is centrally managed and defined? Do teachers possess a body of knowledge highly valued by society? Does the increased role for parents and governors in school choice and governance, respectively, detract from the role of teachers as knowledgeable professionals?'[28]

There was a more contemporary view in Chapter Two, with Harry Cayton's opinion that in the medical profession, professional autonomy had already gone – for two reasons. While the first reason was due to the very complexity of applying knowledge – people can't do it well if they try to do it alone – the second reason was similar to the experience in education: because of the external imposition of standards, guidelines and regulations. The first can involve professional empowerment by choosing to adapt professional practice to working in teams and networking. Whereas the second can be professionally *dis*-empowering: we have seen how the autonomy of school leaders and teachers has gradually become eroded as central government has sought to influence the system of schooling and the practice of teachers.

A university colleague of mine had earlier in his career been a teacher at primary level. I remember him telling me about receiving an e-mail from a former pupil. She'd spotted his name on the university website and got in touch to ask if he was the same Mr Brown who had taught her in Year Five. She hoped he was, because for a long time she'd wanted to tell him that Year Five had been the best year of her whole school life, the year she'd enjoyed the most and the year where she felt she learned the most.

My colleague's pleasure in relating this message was very clear. And it also cast him in a reflective mood. 'That was a good year altogether' he recalled. 'We'd latch onto something that fired the kid's interest, and we'd follow it through over maybe three days'. Then wistfully, 'Course, you wouldn't be able to do that nowadays'.

The real sadness is the effect the restriction of professional autonomy has had on the experience of school learning for young people. The lessening of opportunities to be responsive to young peoples' learning needs has stifled young people's natural enjoyment of learning. There's been widespread condemnation of the fact that external pressures and directives have inevitably led to teachers 'teaching to the test', and Guy Claxton points out that while this may have influenced an increase in levels of reading *ability*, it has been at a cost. Despite the Harry Potter phenomenon, reading *enjoyment* has gone down. Research to evaluate the effect of the National Literacy Strategy found that pleasure in reading stories for eleven-year-old boys fell from 70 per cent in 1998 to 55 per cent in 2003. While girls' enjoyment held up better, since 2003 their pleasure in reading stories has dropped to nearer the boys' level.[29]

'I lead other workers in my classroom, but in the department – as much as you'd like to lead, so much gets in the way. Accountability curtails your autonomy at whatever level you're working at. Leaders have to have confidence to make difficult decisions, based on evidence, within the requirements of autonomy'.

Janet – Primary teacher

'The most worrying thing is there's a danger that modern teachers are not trained, prepared, to propose their own change. The scope of teacher innovation is limited due to the highly prescriptive nature of the curriculum. There is more in higher education than in schools, but HE has a lot of irritating bureaucracy. In HE there are flexible working hours, and you can determine your own curriculum – which is worth a lot. This ought to be available in schools'.

Richard – Primary School Headteacher

'There's a need to break down artificial barriers – allow learners to learn at their own pace.'

David – Director of an Institute for Applied Education Research

So the balancing act is achieving a level of individual autonomy whereby leaders and teachers can practice creatively within the boundaries of accountability, and where learners can develop their individuality within the requirements of national standards of education – and both can flourish within time constraints. Which plainly is not a simple matter. Neither is it a new dilemma. In his biography of the Victorian philosopher and social reformer John Stuart Mill, Richard Reeves describes how it was an issue that engaged Mill at an intellectual and also a practical level:

'...for Mill, the litmus test of any social reform, school curriculum or political arrangement was the degree to which they would enhance or erode autonomy. The social reformers of the age worried about how to get workers more food, money, leisure and health. Mill worried about how to get them more freedom.'[30]

The balancing act: Time control vs autonomy

This chapter invites you to consider your work as a leader in the context of systems. It involves a shift away from straightforward 'cause and effect' thinking to try and understand how strategies derived from linear thinking may not always achieve the intended outcome, even with the best of intentions. Like the Reversing Falls or the Severn Bore, unintended outcomes can occur because of a combination of influencing factors.

The chapter also invited you to consider two features of the education system that both influence each other, and impact upon educational outcomes. The organisation and time-frame of schooling is often taken as a 'given'; something inviolate that may be tinkered with but the rationale rarely questioned. How the timetable impacts upon teacher autonomy in developing their creativity, and the creativity of their students, is just one of the dynamics within the system that affects educational outcomes.

CREATIVE LEADERSHIP THINKING SPACE

- What initiatives could a creative leader introduce to incorporate flexibility into timetabling?

- How might a creative leader stimulate teacher autonomy within the boundaries of accountability?

Notes

1 Peter Senge 1990:66
2 *Ibid.* 1990:73
3 Joseph O'Connor and Ian McDermott 1997:xvii
4 *Ibid.* 1997:18
5 Guy Claxton 2008:45–6
6 Anushka Asthana 2007
7 *The Cost of Inclusion* The Princes Trust 2007:9
8 *Ibid.* 2007:8
9 Department for Education NEET Statistics – Quarterly Brief – Quarter 2, 2011
10 *The Cost of Inclusion* The Princes Trust 2007:9
11 *Ibid.* 2007:8

12 *Child poverty in perspective: An overview of child well-being in rich countries.* UNICEF 2007

13 Michael Fullan 2004:5

14 Neil Tweedie (2010) quoting Anastasia de Waal, Director of Education for Civitas.

15 Guy Claxton 2008:23

16 Sir Ken Robinson 2001:24

17 Guy Claxton 2008:52. The assembly line analogy has also been described elsewhere, for example Hedley Beare (2006) *How we Envisage Schooling in the 21st Century*, SSAT: London; Peter Senge et al. (2000) *Schools that Learn,* Nicolas Brealey: London.

18 Guy Claxton 2008:17

19 Sir Ken Robinson 2001:24

20 Joseph O'Connor and Ian McDermott 1997:252

21 Ibid. 1997:32

22 Malcolm Gladwell 2000:259

23 Joseph O'Connor and Ian McDermott 1997:84

24 Michael Fullan 2004:8

25 Tsuey-Ping Lee 2007

26 Chris Roycroft-Davis *A self-made man. Daily Express,* Thursday 10 June 2010, p.13

27 Richard Reeves 2001:133

28 Lesley Kydd 1997:113

29 Guy Claxton 2008:19, citing research by Rebecca Clarkson and Marian Sainsbury 2007.

30 Richard Reeves 2007:174

4

What is Education For?

This chapter suggests the key question for leadership in education is defining the purpose of education. The chapter explores different notions in this respect, and suggests that there are claims on education that often conflict, and which can create tensions that a leader has to balance. As Guy Claxton has written, the biggest worry is not that schools are failing in their own terms; it is that their terms of reference are antiquated and constricted. Getting to the root of the problem needs going back to the fundamental purpose of education to ask what schools are for.[1]

A young couple were telling me about their experience at parents' evening at the end of their son's first year at comprehensive school. They had looked forward to it with anticipation; their son had been an avid reader from a very young age so they had every reason to believe there would be some positive comments from his teachers.

The teachers all agreed their son was indeed above average intelligence; he shone in class discussions and his knowledge was impressive for his age. But there was a sting in the tail: when it came to committing his thoughts and knowledge to paper they could barely coax a few sentences from him. 'Until they bring out an oral exam', remarked one teacher, 'I can't see him passing. He just won't write enough'. 'And after all', added this particular teacher, 'my job is to get him to pass exams'.

I pondered about that comment later. I wondered whether it was merely a chance remark by the teacher aimed at stressing the importance of passing exams to the couple and their son. Or rather was it an indicator of a mindset that saw his role in education as just that: teaching young people to pass exams?

It's probably not a question that engages busy teachers too much during the demands of their everyday work. But the question 'What is Education for?' is at the core of leadership at any level. A principal may excel at managing an institution, organizing the timetable and curriculum, planning the budget; a teacher may be efficient in lesson planning and classroom management, but does the answer to that question provide the thrust and energy that flows through the whole institution and drives forward the work of everyone involved? It's a difficult question and the answer is even harder to define, but unless we give it frequent examination we are in danger of having no more than a superficial approach to what education can, or should, be. Not only do we have to try to find the solution, we have to question our assumptions if we want to aspire to call ourselves 'educators'. As John Wilson puts it, we cannot just assume because we are involved in teaching or leading a school, that we are involved in education:

'We may call certain things 'schools' and certain people 'teachers': and we may say that what we are doing is to educate children, but we have to be able to show that this is, in fact, what we are doing. The mere existence of social practices with the word 'education' attached to them indicates nothing; any more than, in the police state of Orwells' *Nineteen Eighty-Four* (1949), the existence of an institution called 'The Ministry of Truth' proved that the institution was, in fact, concerned with truth (rather than, as Orwell represents it, with propaganda).'[2]

CREATIVE LEADERSHIP THINKING SPACE

Consider your initial personal response to the question 'What is Education For?'

The trouble is that education is an emotive subject, one on which everyone tends to have a view. And it's similar when you try to define teaching. I've heard teachers remark that everyone thinks they would know how to teach. It's not that teaching is held in low regard as being an easy option, rather it's because we've all experienced schooling of some sort or another so we think we know how it should be done. We may not have had a spell in hospital, we may not have had an encounter with the law, so our views on the health or legal systems will not necessarily be informed by personal experience. But our view of teaching will be, because we've all experienced it and we know what worked – or didn't work – for us. By extension, I guess our view of education as a whole will also be tempered by our experience, and perhaps that's one reason why the purpose of education can encompass so many differing views, and can tend to be such a contentious issue.

But one thing theorists seem to agree on, is that leadership needs to promote a clear vision to be able to align the work of an institution to a common purpose. Given the complexity of the educational project, this is not always as easy as it sounds. For one thing – as you saw in Chapter 3 – the metaphor of a factory production line maintains a tenacious hold against competing attempts to define education differently.

While there may be a tendency to accept practices of previous eras, our view of a proper purpose for education may also be influenced by an overarching ideological framework, developed from a combination of our experience, and absorption by osmosis from our cultural background and upbringing (See Table 1, page 50). But leaders in particular need to check out their assumptions if they are to promote a clear and purposeful vision, one in keeping with their own particular educational context. The teachers' view of his job as 'getting young people to pass exams' is just one perspective. As you will see, there are of course alternatives.

CREATIVE LEADERSHIP THINKING SPACE

What would you say was your personal philosophy on education? Is it primarily concerned with:

- Tradition
- Progression
- Enterprise
- Social Reconstruction

Education as delivering a curriculum

The system of schooling has indeed proved to be remarkably resistant to change (see Chapter 3). While the structure and practice of schooling remains substantially the same, perhaps the most protected element has been the curriculum.

Table 1 – Educational Ideologies

	Key Points
Traditionalism	• Rooted in a belief in the value of a cultural and disciplinary heritage, of which academics are custodians. The role of schools is to transmit this heritage to the next generation who are expected to receive it passively and gratefully. • Elitism is justified in terms of the inherent difficulties of achieving a good education and the limited distribution of talent in society. • The content of subjects is vitally important • Teachers are custodians of a great heritage
Progressivism	• Claims to be 'student-centred', in the sense of valuing students' participation in planning, delivering, assessing and evaluating • Students' freedom of choice and personal development take priority over subject knowledge • Rejects elitism and favours mass access to higher education. The role of education is to give a 'step up' to disadvantaged individuals in the largest numbers possible
Enterprise	• Education is primarily concerned with developing people to be good and efficient workers • New technology and new approaches to teaching and learning are valued both as more efficient and effective tools than traditional approaches, and for their development of important skills in students • There is emphasis on transferable 'core skills': communication, IT, literacy, etc.
Social Reconstructionism	• Claims that education can be a force for positive social change, including for creating improved individuals who can critically address prevailing social norms and help change them for the better • Shares a change ideology with Enterprise, but the nature of the desired change different and more radical • Shares a preference of active, problem-solving pedagogy with Progressivism • Favours a focus on subject disciplines, autonomous learning, but with strong guidance from a teachers, together with an emphasis on emancipatory and critical projects, as well as on personal development

Extract from Paul Trowler (2002). Reproduced by kind permission of the publisher Taylor and Francis Books (UK)

Sir Ken Robinson says that the UK system, like many systems in Europe, starts from the premise that there are ten subjects in the world and we devise a system of education to teach them.[3] Since education was first introduced in the nineteenth century, the relevant importance of subjects has formed a hierarchy that retains its unquestioned hold: prime importance is attached to Language, Mathematics and Science, then the Humanities, then the Arts.

This hierarchy of subject importance has persisted throughout reforms of the system to meet the labour needs of an industrial economy. The model adopted by many European countries in the post-war period provided separate educational provision for the 20 per cent destined for professional roles from the 80 per cent heading for manual work. Yet the assumptions of the curriculum clung on limpet-like, with the 80 per cent heading for secondary modern schools receiving a watered down version of the grammar school curriculum (Chapter 3 again).

In the UK, pressure began to be exerted on the traditional curriculum during the 1970s and 1980s with efforts to align the school curriculum more explicitly with the needs of the economy. There was an attempt to foster new approaches to teaching and learning with the introduction of the Technical and Vocational Education Initiative (TVEI).[4] Yet there was a tension between this movement and the demand for greater curriculum uniformity that culminated in the overloaded and prescriptive National Curriculum.

By the early 1990s the education community breathed a sigh of relief and gratefully accepted recommendations for substantial slimming down of the National Curriculum content. But Mike Davies and Gwyn Edwards suggest this approval may have been misplaced since the underlying assumptions of the curriculum were never questioned. The underlying structure survived virtually intact with – not surprisingly – the arts and humanities being the casualties.[5]

With a curriculum that is predominantly content and knowledge-based it follows that quality assurance methods involve testing and examination to ensure the requisite knowledge has been absorbed. Attempts to ease examination pressure by introducing assessment by coursework have really only nibbled at the edges. The predominant UK government rhetoric over the last few regimes has been concerned with accountability and 'raising standards'. Sir Ken Robinson rails against the 'insistent mantra' of raising standards, since for him the standards were designed for other times and other purposes, and 'we will not navigate through the complex environment of the future by peering relentlessly into a rear view mirror'.[6]

The teachers' view of his role a 'getting young people to pass exams' would also be spot on according to the Principal of Wellington College, Anthony Seldon. Reportedly, his view is that school authorities, schools and teachers are now valued for one thing alone: their success at achieving exam passes.[7]

Along with David James[8], they point out that the obsession with examination grades has created a culture where everything has to be measured and quantified if it is seen to have value. But all this has been done at a cost. In the case of A-levels, they suggest that a 97 per cent pass rate has been achieved on a thin diet: a view supported by five out of six university admission tutors who no longer believe that A-levels promote creative thinking.

Thus the limitations of the perspective 'education as delivering the curriculum' lie in the unquestioning assumptions about a curriculum, which, because of the dominance of content knowledge, relies upon a particular mode of testing of students. And there is a further limitation, in that the testing regime itself aspires to a hierarchy of importance. In this respect, Guy Claxton points out the devastating end result of the thrust towards achieving results:

> '...the message of the educational medium is clear: success means getting enough points at A-level to get onto the university course you want. By that yardstick, three out of every four young adults are going to fail. (2008:9)'

Education as developing learning

While in many ways the concept of 'curriculum' still means 'subject content', there has been a more recent movement in terms of planning content and pedagogy simultaneously, and understanding the relationship between the two.[9] For teachers who see themselves as having a much broader influence on the development of learning in their students, there has been a whole plethora of new ideas on how learning generally can be stimulated.

Developments in cognitive neuroscience and brain imaging have spawned a 'brain-friendly learning' movement based on the way the brain is naturally designed to learn. Eric Jensen, an enthusiast in this area, claims that the brain does not learn on demand by a school's rigid, inflexible timetable. What was thought of as critical in the past may not be very important at all, and perhaps past instructional methods really emerged because they were measurable.[10] Rather, 'brain-friendly learning' advocates accommodating the unique features of the individual student within a holistic approach that takes account of the learning environment, the impact of emotional state, motivation and physiology on learning. In practical terms, the approach offers strategies to aid learning such as 'mind-mapping', creating a multi-sensory learning environment, helping young people to get into the right 'state' for learning.

There has also been a movement away from the idea that we all think and learn in the same way. Most teachers will have encountered the notion of visual, auditory and kinaesthetic (VAK) preferences in thinking and learning. For many, VAK has offered a shared vocabulary with which to discuss their individual learning styles with students. Many schools have taken up Howard Gardner's concept of 'multiple intelligences' (MI)[11] that has moved away from the notion of a single fixed entity, to use the word 'intelligence' to describe a range of human abilities. While education has traditionally placed highest value on the abilities to read, write and communicate with words (linguistic intelligence) and to reason and calculate (logical/mathematical intelligence), Gardner adds a further five 'intelligences': musical (music smart), spatial and visual (picture smart), kinaesthetic (body smart), interpersonal (people smart) and intrapersonal (self smart), with a sixth added after further research – naturalist (nature smart). Following these principles, many 'multiple intelligence schools' have been set up worldwide with the aim of fostering and developing the full range of 'smartness' in their students.

Teaching is a demanding occupation, and teachers will naturally grasp at emerging ideas that offer strategies to encourage their students learning. But for every movement there is a counter movement, and there has been criticism of both of the usefulness of the strategies and even the basis of the claim for the existence of different 'learning styles'. Guy Claxton, for instance, admits that teachers will be keen to learn more about learning in order to teach their pupils better, but writes scathingly about a needless misrepresentation of science. Neuroscience is in its infancy and ideas such as drinking water in class because a dehydrated brain learns less effectively are reducing things to a much too simplistic level. And he's generally sceptical about 'brain-friendly learning' because there is no good evidence that the strategies make any difference to students measured performance on anything.[12]

As well as a concern about making unsubstantiated claims on the basis of emerging scientific evidence, there has also been criticism of the lack of a coherent theoretical basis. In relation to Gardner's MI theory, Professor John White thinks we should be grateful that he has opened teachers' eyes to new possibilities. However, he also thinks there are dangers in taking MI theory on board, particularly as the seven or eight categories are too close to familiar curricular areas for comfort. There's a danger that we may escape the shackles of IQ intelligence only to find ourselves imprisoned within another dubious theory.[13]

In another very influential report, Frank Coffield and his colleagues reviewed 71 tests used in post-16 education claiming to identify learning styles. They claimed even the most commercially successful tests had low reliability, poor validity, and had a negligible impact on the effectiveness of teaching, and they recommended their use be discontinued.[14] Their main criticism stemmed from the danger that in using the tests, teachers were drawn into labelling students, which was not in the best interests of developing and extending their learning ability.

And of course in practical terms, that has been a very real danger. From my own experience it has been a constant battle – particularly with VAK – to stop teachers referring to visual/auditory/kinaesthetic as though they were fixed and permanent categories (e.g. telling their students 'you *are* a visual learner'). Doing that is no more than reverting to the more or less discredited way we used to think about intelligence – as something that is fixed and immutable. While teachers have grasped materials on learning styles as an opportunity to engage their students in thinking and talking about their learning, regrettably many have missed the point that the real value lies in identifying the less used areas, therefore presenting an opportunity to develop a more well-rounded learning ability. David Hargreaves has pointed out that labelling with a particular style is poor professional practice that can damage a student's learning and development. A good education does not limit young people to a particular style or type, but gives them opportunities to strengthen other learning styles and so broaden their intellectual development.[15]

But the overarching conflict really is between the needs of teachers, who will be looking for 'what works' in relation to developing learning, and theorists who fret about a lack of conceptual coherence. There seems to be a sensible approach to resolution from a research project that has been documenting the experience of teachers engaged in professional development based on neuro-linguistic programming (NLP). NLP is a model that incorporates strategies to aid personal development and relationships and has evolved as a 'community of practice'. Consequently, it lays itself open to accusations of lack of theoretical rigour. The research sponsored by the CfBT Education Trust therefore took a two-fold approach: first, to undertake a systematic literature review of evidence in relation to the impact and use of NLP in education, secondly to record the experiences of teachers trained in NLP in relation to their own development, and the positive impacts on student learning outcomes.

The researchers conclude there is a need for further research evidence on the effects of use of NLP in education practice, and also for a greater conceptual clarity to emerge. Having said that, they also question whether there is really any argument against NLP being taught to teachers before there is more research evidence? Their stance remains:

'...we believe that the qualitative research evidence suggests that there is much that is useful to schools in relation to understanding the nature of influential language as defined by some NLP writing. Teachers have clearly found this useful to influence behaviour and learning in more positive ways whilst preserving the emotional climate in their classroom. It would be a pity to lose this body of knowledge because of poor theoretical explanations about how this works and what is going on when such approaches are applied.'[16]

Perhaps the overarching issue relating to education as developing learning can be summarised with Stephen Pinker's view. Since our genetic and evolutionary inheritance means that we have a predisposition to speak, but no such a predisposition to write or to read, education is a process of compensating for gaps in our biological inheritance and adapting natural predispositions 'to master problems for which they were not designed'.[17]

CREATIVE LEADERSHIP THINKING SPACE

In practice, does your attention focus on delivering a curriculum, or range more towards developing learning generally?

Education as preparation for work

As mentioned earlier, everyone has a view about teaching and education. And a prominent view from employees has been that education should be doing more to prepare young people adequately for the workplace: they point to skills deficits in literacy and numeracy skills in apprentices, and a lack of 'soft skills' and an understanding of the requirements of the workplace in graduates.

I assumed that was a fairly modern dilemma – that is, until the chief executive officer of Colleges Wales John Graystone was telling me about a reforming Member of Parliament at the end of the nineteenth century. Lionel Playfair MP had been to the 1867 Paris Exhibition, and on his return was heard to lament 'the issue upon which there is most unanimity of conviction is that France, Prussia, Austria, Belgium and Switzerland possess good systems of industrial education and that England possesses none'.

So it seems education has long been a battleground where the forces of vocationalism have struggled to attain a foothold in the stronghold of academic dominance. Sir Ken Robinson points to areas of tension that arise from differing priorities. On the one hand, within education, there is the confusion of academic ability with intelligence. Nothing wrong with the promotion of academic ability in itself, the problem lies in the obsessive preoccupation with it. It obscures the fact that there is more to intelligence than academic ability, and more to education than developing it. Even with an acceptance of a linear relationship between general education and employment, that itself creates a further tension: it places schools under pressure to prioritise those subjects that seem most relevant to the economy. Consequently, in most developed countries there is high priority placed on science and technology in schools, with provision for the arts and humanities being cut back. Sir Ken throws doubt over whether this trend is in the best interests of young people or of society in general:

'...it is a mistake to think of the relationship between education and the economy as a straightforward process of supply and demand, like producing biscuits or cars.'[18]

Indeed, the complexity of our modern world has broadened the stance of 'education as preparation for work' from the narrow utilitarian perspective of employers. Sir Ken Robinson recognises that the emphasis on academic learning has tended to value only one way of knowing and, in so doing, has displaced others. Yet, since the economic circumstances in which we now live, and which will be the way of the future, are utterly different from those of 20 or even 10 years ago, we need different styles of education and different priorities.[19] Helena Kennedy Q.C. also echoes the belief that all learning is valuable – 'It has always been difficult to define 'vocational' and 'non-vocational' learning and these concepts are fast becoming less and less valid'.[20]

Helena Kennedy goes further, with a conviction that learning is not only central to economic prosperity, but also to the health of society. The achievement of economic goals and social cohesion are intertwined, with a healthy society being a necessary condition for a thriving economy. Thus many of the skills and qualities required for success at work are the same as those required for success in personal, social and community terms.[21]

> The academic/vocational debate is tired and out-dated. We need to move beyond it. The curriculum needs 'authentic learning' – a stripping away of curriculum subjects to develop a 'philosophy': for 8–14 and 14–19 years.
>
> Professor David Egan

For Sir Ken Robinson of course, the 'philosophy' centres on the development of creativity – in all its forms. It's his view that, up to now, in the interests of the industrial economy and of academic achievement, we have clung to what is only a partial form of education. In doing so we have wasted or destroyed a great deal of what many young people had to offer because its value wasn't recognised. This will not suffice for the complexity of life and work in the twenty-first century:

'The companies, communities and nations that succeed in future will balance their books only by solving the complex equation of human resources. Our own times are being swept along on an avalanche of innovations in science, technology, and social thought. To keep pace with these changes, or to get ahead of them, we will need all our wits about us – literally. We must learn to be creative.[22]

CREATIVE LEADERSHIP THINKING SPACE

To what degree does your philosophy of education include preparation of young people for work?

Education as promoting emotional health and well-being

When international reports record that the UK and USA reach only the bottom third of countries assessed for educational well-being (see Chapter 3) it is not surprising that policy makers have turned their attention to ways that the well-being for children and young people can be encouraged. In the UK government policy includes being healthy, staying safe and achieving economic independence as broad outcomes for the well-being of every child and young person.[23] In Wales particularly, well-being occurs at the core of a School Effectiveness Framework, sharing importance with Improved Learning.[24]

Having worked in Australia, the USA and England, John West-Burnham and his colleagues report that this appears to be a global development. It's a shift that acknowledges that merely 'improving what is' will not meet the challenge of securing excellence and equity for every child. They also note that while for some this change is a liberation from the somewhat exclusive emphasis on the technology of teaching and learning within the classroom, for others it is more of a challenge.[25]

As well as the practical elements of well-being, the trend has accepted the importance of the role of education in promoting and developing emotional health. Emotional health and well-being (EHWB) appears to have been adopted in policy documents as a shorthand term for all aspects of mental health. Guy Claxton notes that, not only has there been a sharp decline in the mental health of teenagers in the last 25 years, surveys and statistics show that more and more young people every year are experiencing fearfulness, self-doubt, self-consciousness and insecurity.[26]

So it's hardly surprising that the increasing prevalence of mental disorders in childhood and adolescence, and their association with detrimental long-term outcomes, has led to a policy agenda that looks to schools to provide early intervention. Given an assumption that there will be a reliance upon teachers and other school staff to be deliverers, or even drivers of the work of EHWB, Judi Kidger and her colleagues interviewed staff at eight secondary schools in England to find out how such work fitted in the broader goals of schools. Amongst the diversity of views was a unanimous belief that EHWB was intimately related to the process of growing up, and as such was inseparable from learning and achieving good learning outcomes. Thus, for some, it was seen as part and parcel of everyone's teaching: just by being in a relationship with pupils, teachers would inevitably have an impact on their emotional health through the way they responded to them. On the other hand, some school staff felt that many teachers were reluctant to focus on this area, either being afraid it would interfere with their core academic duties or because they did not have the emotional energy or necessary knowledge to do so.[27]

Of course EHWB in education is part of a broad overarching trend that acknowledges the impact of emotions upon human ability and behaviour generally. Daniel Goleman admits that he had to wait to write his best-selling book on emotional intelligence until the scientific evidence was sufficiently credible. The place of feelings in mental health research had been surprisingly neglected over the years, despite the fact that the welter of self-help books bore witness to an intuitive sense that emotional responses could be managed. Goleman claimed that developments in brain mapping now enabled science to speak with authority about the irrational aspects of the psyche, and that it also offered a challenge:

'...a challenge to those who subscribe to a narrow view of intelligence, arguing that IQ is a genetic given that cannot be changed by life experience, and that our destiny in life is largely fixed by these aptitudes. That argument ignores the more challenging question: What *can* we change that will help our children fare better in life? What factors are at play, for example, when people of high IQ flounder and those of modest IQ do surprisingly well? I would argue that the difference quite often lies in the abilities called here *emotional intelligence*, which include self-control, zeal and persistence, and the ability to motivate oneself. And these skills [ ] can be taught to children, giving them a better chance to use whatever intellectual potential the genetic lottery may have given them.'[28]

There has indeed been a reorientation towards a more holistic approach in focusing more on the individual learning needs of children and young people.

Richard Churches and John West-Burnham suggest the policy of 'personalised learning' in England implies a need for a substantial empowerment of the learner – even though there had been no clear and coherent definition of personalised learning. And even given that one of the challenging aspects of developments in England has been the lack of any consensus even about the nature of learning. Nevertheless, they think a policy component defined in 2005 by the (then) Department for Education and Skills is worthy of note in that it requires:

'...creative approaches to school organisation, to enable a student-centred approach which integrates performance with wellbeing and inclusive approaches with attainment.'

Plainly there's an indicator here that personalised learning involves more that a narrow 'schooling' approach with an emphasis on targets and outcomes. As Richard and John point out, there's the implication of a focus on the 'affective dimension' as much as any other aspect of organisation life. And this implies a broader and more inclusive model of education.[29]

This broadening of education has included strategies such as the practice of 'Circle Time' in primary schools, aimed at encouraging young children to understand and deal with emotions, as well as developing social and inter-personal skills. The fact that Circle Time evolved from the success of quality circles in industry flags up the intimate relationship between education and the workplace. For Daniel Goleman, the skills of emotional intelligence constitute the 'new rules' of the workplace, and emotional intelligence (EI) is therefore a crucial factor if education is to prepare young people for the new world of work:

'For our children, this includes an education in emotional literacy; for those already at work, it means cultivating our emotional competence. All this, of course, demands rethinking the notion of the 'basics' in education: Emotional intelligence is now as crucial to our children's future as the standard academic fare'.[30]

The 'basics' of education were quite dramatically referred to by Anthony Seldon in his lecture to the College of Teachers. He claimed the twenty-first century obsession with teaching 'facts' harked back to Thomas Gradgrinds' utilitarian values in Dickens's *Hard Times*, which resulted in a system that stifled imagination, individuality and flair. Further, Dickens's message is as timely and urgent for us as it was in 1854:

'It is that soulless, loveless, desiccated education damages children for a lifetime. Education should be an opening of the heart and mind. That is what education means; it is this, or it is nothing'.[31]

CREATIVE LEADERSHIP THINKING SPACE

In what ways does your practice include education in emotional literacy, and influencing the well-being of young people generally?

Education as preparation for citizenship and democracy

It's not just in current times that we experience a tension between the competing demands on education. Education policy in England and Wales has been a swinging pendulum that has regularly drawn attention from a focus on producing a suitably educated workforce, to advocating a wider socialisation and developmental purpose for the education system.

Economist J. K. Galbraith had commented that, because a modern economy required a well-prepared, adaptable labour force, education made education economically essential. However, a line had to be drawn:

> 'The good society cannot accept that education in the modern economy is primarily in the service of economics, it has a larger political and social role, a yet deeper justification in itself'.[32]

The social role has also been influenced by the tendency in the UK to regard young people as a sort of social barometer, with their behaviour seen as symptoms of wider social ills. At the end of the twentieth century, rising numbers of births to teenagers, increased delinquency and violence, teenage drinking and violence were taken as indicators of moral decline, and there was also a concern at a lack of interest in voting and party politics. Globally as well as locally, it could be seen that wider forces were reshaping society. As a response to national and international concerns, notions of citizenship and individual rights emerged to influence ideas about the moral purpose of education.[33]

A response to this trend was a UK government sponsored report on 'Education for Citizenship and the teaching of democracy in Schools' with the result that education for citizenship became a new and compulsory subject for secondary pupils in England from 2002. Given the traditional nature of the school system, I suppose it was inevitable that the response would be for citizenship to be something to be 'taught'. However, the vision was much more than an additional compulsory school subject: the core of citizenship was envisaged as its 'active' component:

'We aim at no less than a change in the political culture of this country both nationally and locally: for people to think of themselves as active citizens, willing, able and equipped to have an influence in public life and with the critical capacities to weigh evidence before speaking and acting; to build on and to extend radically to young people the best in existing traditions of community involvement and public service, and to make them individually confident in finding new forms of involvement and action among themselves'.[34]

This 'action-orientated' approach is echoed by the Citizenship Foundation, where citizenship education is envisaged as enabling people to make their own decisions and to take responsibility for their own lives and their communities. Significantly, the Foundation also sees the role of schools as not simply teaching citizenship, but demonstrating it through the way they operate.[35]

Indeed, it's not only what young people are taught but also their actual experiences at school that contribute to their understanding of their role as future citizens, and in this respect a democratic school ethos is influential.[36] The past ten years has seen the creation of opportunities for children and young people to have their voice heard. Membership of a school council, taking part in an interview process for a new headteacher, are now experiences available to young pupils. Initiatives such as *Learner Voice* seek to involve young people in shaping their own educational experiences.[37] Whether these initiatives are changing the ethos of schooling, or paying lip service to the notion of developing active citizenship is still an open question. Because as J. K. Galbraith points out, democracy is a demanding thing: education about citizenship and democracy not only brings into existence a population with an understanding of active citizenship, it also creates their demand to be heard.[38]

Which is probably a concern that underpins the school of thought that democracy simply cannot work in schools. Many believe that democracy is a right of adults, but not of young people. And as Michael Apple and James Beane have pointed out, despite the commonsense idea that young people need to experience a democratic way of life to be able to understand what it means, schools have been remarkably undemocratic institutions:

'While democracy emphasizes cooperation among people, too many schools have fostered competition [ ] While democracy depends on caring for the common good, too many schools [ ] have emphasised an idea of individuality based almost entirely on self-interest. While democracy prizes diversity, too many schools have largely reflected the interests and aspirations of the most powerful groups in this country and ignored those of the less powerful. While schools in a democracy would presumably demonstrate how to achieve equal opportunity for all, too many schools are plagued with structures such as tracking and ability grouping that deny equal opportunity and results to many, particularly the poor, people of colour and women.'[39]

It's not that there hasn't been a willingness from governments to tackle social inequalities. Headteacher of Phoenix High School Sir William Atkinson feels successive governments in Britain the US have had the laudable goal of improving the education attainment of all their students, but especially those drawn from the lowest performing sections of the population. However, regrettably, for the vast majority of white working class students – and those drawn from ethnic minorities – the achievement gap in the UK remains unacceptably wide, and, on current rates of improvement, will take many decades before there is any sense of parity. In the meantime, lives and communities will continue to be blighted.[40]

CREATIVE LEADERSHIP THINKING SPACE

How does your establishment demonstrate democratic principles in the way it operates?

The balancing act

What the different perspectives demonstrate is that there has been more and more requirements made of education, and increasing expectations upon the role of teachers in educating young people. The fact that teaching has evolved to be a demanding and – for some – stressful occupation reflects the multi-faceted nature of education in the twenty-first century. Many would say the expectations are too high; that education can't be expected to fulfil all of society's needs, that teachers can't be all things to all people.

But life itself is now immensely more complex than even 50 years ago. If education is for anything, surely its role must be to prepare young people for their future. Given that we don't know what that future will be, the best preparation for their future will be that all young people are equipped to learn about their world, and acquire the attributes they will need to navigate their way successfully through their life experiences. If that is the case, all of the purposes for education impact upon each other: which serves to remind us of the frequently quoted view of John Dewey that education is not a preparation for life, but life itself.

A challenge for education? Certainly. And Mike Davies and Gwyn Edwards articulate the balancing act that leadership in education will need to achieve:

'Whether we like it or not, education is caught up in the turbulence of exponential change the outcomes of which are beyond prediction. Therefore the principal purpose of education should be helping young people acquire the dispositions, skills, understandings and values that will enable them to live their lives intelligently, meaningfully, constructively and cooperatively in the midst of complexity, uncertainty and instability they will increasingly encounter. There is no sense in a curriculum designed to predict and control in a world that is in a state of constant flux. What is required is a curriculum rationale that seeks to rediscover the intrinsic purposes and principles of education, and that give schools the freedom and incentive to respond flexibly, creatively and responsibly to the needs of their pupils in an uncertain and rapidly changing world.'[41]

CREATIVE LEADERSHIP THINKING SPACE

Think back to your first response to the question 'What is Education for?' In what ways has your view changed since reading this chapter?

Notes

1 Guy Claxton 2008:27
2 John Wilson 2000:5
3 Sir Ken Robinson 2001:196
4 Mike Davies and Gwyn Edwards 2001:98
5 *Ibid.* 2001:98
6 Sir Ken Robinson 2001:16
7 *The Observer,* 8 March 2009
8 *The Independent,* 14 July 2009
9 See the report by the General Teaching Council for England 'Creating a Curriculum for Learning' available at http://www.gtce.org.uk/documents/publicationpdfs/creating_a_curriculum accessed 4 September 2009
10 Eric Jensen 2008:4
11 Howard Gardner 1983
12 Guy Claxton 2008:48–49
13 John White 1998:35

14 Frank Coffield et al. 2004
15 David Hargreaves 2005:11–12
16 John Carey et al. 2010:30–1
17 Stephen Pinker 2002:223
18 Sir Ken Robinson 2001:7–9
19 *Ibid.* 2001:200
20 Helena Kennedy 1998:164
21 *Ibid.* 1998:163–164
22 Sir Ken Robinson 2001:203
23 *Every Child Matters* in England, the *10 Entitlements of Young People* in Wales.
24 Department for Children, Education, Lifelong Learning and Skills, Welsh Assembly Government 2008
25 John West-Burnham et al. 2007:5
26 Guy Claxton 2008:2
27 Judi Kidger et al. 2010:919–935
28 Daniel Goleman 1996:xi–xii
29 Richard Churches and John West-Burnham 2008:8
30 Daniel Goleman 1998:313
31 Anthony Seldon's inaugural lecture as professor of education to the College of Teachers, reported in *The Observer*, 16 August 2009
32 J. K. Galbraith 1996:69
33 Jacquie Turnbull 2002:124
34 Qualifications and Curriculum Authority 1998:8
35 http://www.citizenshipfoundation.org.uk accessed 24 July 2009
36 Jagdish Gundara 2000:14
37 http://www.niace.org.uk/curreent-work/area/learner-voice
38 J. K. Galbraith 1996:71
39 Michael Apple and James Beane 1999:13–14
40 Sir William Atkinson 2009:7
41 Mike Davies & Gwyn Edwards 2001:104–5

5

Seeking Solutions in Leadership as Creativity

This chapter takes creativity from the realm of artistic endeavour and asks you to consider it as a function of intelligence that is evident in everyday individual resourcefulness. It sets up a challenge for you to consider how you can develop your leadership in responding creatively to everyday issues. As John Adair has written, it's not what happens to you in life that matters but how you respond: the creative response is to transform bad things into good, problems into opportunities.[1]

Have you ever noticed how people have certain phrases they tend to use regularly? Sometimes they become so predictable you can almost anticipate what they're going to say. I was once on a committee where the officers in attendance used to play their own secret game of bingo – they used to tick off every time they heard a favoured phrase uttered by the members and see who could spot the most.

Sometimes it can become irritating because you get a sense that dependence upon a particular stock phrase becomes a substitute for thinking more creatively. My colleague Michael for instance – we'd be having what seemed to be a fruitful discussion on a management issue when he would come out with 'Of course the problem I have is...' Similarly with Neil when we worked on a research project together, his favoured line was 'The difficulty I have is...'

Not content with allowing such phrases to sound the death knell of further creative thought, my response was usually 'So if that's the problem/difficulty, what's the solution?'

You'll probably find, if you try this yourself, that the initial reaction can be negative: when people have adopted a problem/difficulty focus it can become a barrier to working their way through to a solution. For whatever reason – finding a solution would take too much hard work, we haven't the resources, we haven't the time, people wouldn't accept it, etc., etc. – remaining stuck at the problem/difficulty stage can be a useful comfort zone.

But psychologist Robert Sternberg says creative leaders do not hit their heads against the wall when they cannot solve problems; to a large extent, people *decide* to be creative. They exhibit a creative attitude towards life – they redefine and reformulate problems they cannot solve:

> 'If the best possible outcome is not that good, or the worst possible outcome unacceptably bad, or the expected outcome inadequate, one should look for another solution.'[2]

Finding solutions to everyday problems is only one aspect of creativity. The ability to recognize where problems exist is another. The first part of this book set about exploring tensions that exist in education systems that restrict the development of creative thinking and approaches. These are tensions that creative leaders need to handle, without dismissing them as 'the difficulty I have...'.

However, if you're looking for a definitive model of creativity in educational leadership, you won't find it in this book. Not only is a concept of 'one size fits all' incompatible with a notion of creativity, there are just too many variables – in educational contexts, social environments, practitioners, cohorts of students – to be able to envisage how a single model can be applicable to all circumstances. Each person's creativity is individual to them; a complex dynamic of personal skills, values and culture that results in an expression of something novel within a particular context.[3] That's why Howard Gardner claims creativity is not a single entity, and that the claim of psychologists that it can be measured by psychometric tests is too narrow a definition.[4] Mark Runco agrees, and has provided a neat description of the multi-faceted nature of creativity:

'Creativity is notoriously difficult to define and measure. This is probably because it is complex, with various forms of expression, and because it is overdetermined, with multiple potential influences. Creativity is certainly not the same thing as intelligence or giftedness. Like creativity, these may involve problem solving, but sometimes it is better to look at creativity as a kind of self-expression, and sometimes it involves problem finding in addition to problem solving'.[5]

Nevertheless, despite its complexity, I believe we can tease out some overarching principles relating to creativity. But before doing that, we have to acknowledge that, regrettably, creativity is a notion that comes with baggage. Tim Smit suggests some may be wary of it because of a suggestion of genius, for others it may hint at dodgy accounting practices.[6] So perhaps a first step needs to be to challenge certain assumptions about creativity, and to clarify what creativity *is not*.

Creativity is ... not totally about free expression

This is probably one of the major misconceptions that cause concern about creativity in education. It's associated with an image of chaotic classrooms, children running riot, lack of control. It harks back to a short-lived '*laissez-faire*' trend in the 1970s when certain 'progressive' schools were castigated by government for lack of formal teaching and learning.

The idea of free expression is also associated with artistic endeavours: we tend to think about 'artistic' people using their particular medium to express their individuality. Yet all artistic expression is actually only achieved following lengthy and disciplined labour. Individuals may be fortunate to be born with a talent in a particular area, but that talent comes to nothing without the application to control their medium: the many hours of practice to master a musical instrument, the nurturing of techniques to produce works of art and sculpture, the discipline of many lonely hours to produce works of literature.

For educators, maintaining the discipline of a large class of students, while at the same time encouraging their individual creativity to flourish, can appear a daunting, if not impossible, task. Yet creative teachers consistently achieve this. Phil Beadle is an English teacher, a previous winner of the UK's National Teaching Award as Secondary Teacher of the Year, and a double Royal Television Society Award winning broadcaster for the TV series 'The Unteachables' and 'Can't Read Can't Write'. So you could say he is a high profile example of a creative teacher.

There was a particularly compelling image on one of his television programmes of Phil getting a group of stroppy adolescents to read Shakespeare to a herd of cows. With such a flamboyant style, it may then come as a bit of a surprise to read his book *How to Teach*, and find the first chapter entitled 'Management of Students'. The first rule – 'Turn up. Take the punches. Smile back' – is encouraging. Most teachers will have experienced the nightmare scenario of the class from hell where it took all their professional resilience to face them on a Monday morning. Phil's following advice is equally precise: rigorous implementation of seating, Stalinist application of rules about coats off, bags off tables, insistence on students looking at you when you speak, even insistence that all students put their pens down before you speak.[7] (I worried a bit about that last one. We all run different thinking processes, and for years I've been advising practitioners that some students need to move around or fiddle with something to be able to think. But then I realised that Phil was writing about directing students' attention when the teacher is giving necessary instruction, not about times when they're working on a task. So plainly the two are not mutually exclusive).

At first glance, rigorous application of rules and creative teaching may not appear to fit comfortably together. Yet, in leadership we can find another example of these two apparently ill-matched bedfellows. Sir Michael Wilshaw started his career as a headteacher by transforming a school earmarked for closure into an establishment hailed for its outstanding results. He then moved to become the first head of Mossbourne Community Academy in Hackney, one of London's more deprived boroughs. As its first head, Michael Wilshaw not only created the school's educational philosophy, he also helped the architect in the design of the buildings. Mossbourne, reportedly, became Wilshaw's 'personal creation'.[8] Yet he outlines an ethos of rigid discipline: rules on uniform and length of hair, visits to fast food shops banned, breaches of discipline punished by detention on the same day or even on Saturdays.

What this combination of creativity and discipline helps us to do is be clearer about the difference between creativity and innovation – two concepts that can often be used interchangeably. Roland Bel suggests that a good 'innovation' leader is characterised by the ability to excel in the apparently conflicting skills of creativity and discipline. Creativity is recognising opportunities, innovation is developing them.[9] Or as an illustration from the corporate world puts it:

'Creativity is the mental and social process – fuelled by conscious or unconscious insight – of generating ideas, concepts, and associations. Innovation is the successful exploitation of new ideas: it is a profitable outcome of the creative process...'[10]

Plainly the aim of education is not the same as producing innovated new products as in the corporate world. But education still seeks a 'profitable' outcome: for the benefit of the individual student, and for society as a whole. Phil's creative teaching and disciplined approach produces learning for students who have managed to evade the experience previously. Michael Wilshaw's 'creation' placed Mossbourne amongst the top three dozen comprehensives with 85 per cent of pupils achieving national target grades at GCSE.[11] Both outcomes can be termed innovative: the development of new ways of doing things to creative original outcomes.

Within education, the notion that creativity and a disciplined approach cannot be compatible also comes from lack of clarity about the difference between *behavioural* freedom and *psychological* freedom. The ultimate outcome of encouraging behavioural freedom is anarchy, whereas nurturing psychological freedom provides a seedbed for creativity. As Robert Fisher puts it:

> 'Psychological freedom fosters creativity by permitting children freedom of expression. Children's behaviour needs to have limits and be moulded to the needs of society but their symbolic expression need not be so circum-scribed. Children should feel secure enough to try out new things and be given the freedom to do so, within bounds. Their freedom of expression should not inhibit the freedom of others. In a creative climate, adults and children value originality rather than conformity, not the sameness but the difference of ideas.'[12]

CREATIVE LEADERSHIP THINKING SPACE

• What do you think of the idea that creativity needs a disciplined approach to produce innovation?

• What would be an example from your own experience of creativity + discipline = innovation?

The association of creativity with free expression does not just occur in relation to the education of children. Sir Ken Robinson refers to this misconception being reinforced by the popularity on management courses of using techniques such as brainstorming as a way of generating a flow of ideas. Generating ideas may be part of the creative process but it isn't that easy; if it was there wouldn't be any need for special techniques. Yet as in the example below illustrates, inexpert use of techniques can also result in a Missed Opportunity, and can stifle creativity, rather than stimulate it.

Missed opportunity

At my university we had one of those whole-day faculty planning meetings. New initiatives were being proposed by management, and after receiving the party line in plenary we were split into teams to work out our action plans. There'd been plenty of information to get us thinking. My brain was buzzing with ideas: I was already chatting with colleagues on the way to the break out rooms on how we could take the proposals forward in our team.

So as we gathered in the room we'd been allocated, we were all geared up to firm up our ideas on the new initiatives. We arranged the chairs into a circle and looked expectantly to our team leader to start us off on action planning. Paul hadn't seemed to recognize the level of energy in the group. Then I remembered he was fresh from a three-day training course in group counselling techniques, and plainly, he was still mulling over the techniques. Unfortunately, he also couldn't wait to put them into practice. Misjudging the climate in the room completely, he leant back in his chair, gazed at the ceiling with his fingers forming a pyramid and mused 'So I think we'll just take some time...some time to think about things in general...let's just have some free thinking...let's just have some time where anyone can say whatever comes into their head'.

If you wanted to think up a good way to derail a creative process I don't think you could have come up with a better strategy. We'd already been through the thinking process; what we needed now was to capture the ideas and work out how they could be converted into action. The sharing of ideas can be a risky business, and we were looking to Paul to guide and facilitate this stage of the process. But it felt like we were being taken back to the starting post when we'd already run half the race. The overall effect was a stunned and uncomfortable silence. Unable to build on the energy and ideas in the room, all Paul had succeeded in doing was halting a process that had already started.

Creativity is ... not restricted to certain people

One of the reasons we exist as the cleverest creatures on our planet is the fact that we have been able to consistently adapt to our environment. Our evolution has equipped us with the physical and mental capacity to make creative use of resources available to us. In Darwinian terms, it's not the strongest species that survives, but the most adaptable.

That being the case, when we think about the many forms of human ingenuity that have ensured our survival, how can there be any doubt that creativity is not a universal and innate capacity? Which is not the same as saying we all have the same type of creative capacity, because plainly people have unique and different talents. But for Sir Ken Robinson, there is no doubt about the universality of creativity:

'Creativity is not a separate faculty that some people have and others do not. It is a function of intelligence: it takes many forms, it draws from many different capacities and we all have different creative capabilities. Creativity is possible in any activity in which human intelligence is actively engaged'.[13]

If we accept that creativity is not restricted to certain people, it leads us to Abraham Maslow's question 'Why in God's name isn't everyone creative?' And – as many others have – we can be drawn to respond to that challenge by questioning whether our system of schooling is designed to maximise the creative capacity of children, young people, and indeed of adults who work in the system. In this respect, it's worth reflecting on the findings of a MORI poll carried out for the Campaign for Learning in 2000, 2002 and 2004, which asked over 2,000 11–16 years old to name the three most common activities in their classrooms. Note that these were not the youngest pupils, rather students of an age where you might expect a need for classroom activities to be of a style to stimulate and engage the adolescent brain. Yet as Guy Claxton has summarised the findings:

'Number one across all three surveys was 'copying from a board or book', selected by an average of 60 per cent of the same. It is worth noting that the situation is actually deteriorating as 'copying down' rose from 56 per cent in 2000 to 61 per cent in 2004. Two of the other most common activities were 'listen to the teacher talking for a long time', and 'take notes while my teacher talks'. The least likely thing to happen in a classroom according to the students surveyed was 'learn things that relate to the real world.'[14]

Robert Fisher agrees that all children are born with creative ability, but it is up to us to provide a climate that supports the child's creative efforts.[15] Anna Craft has also written that creativity is an essential life skill, which needs to be fostered by the education system.[16] Sadly, the research cited above suggests that the experience of a climate that fosters their creative capacity has not been available to all young people. The poll is suggestive of a presumption that 'learning' is what young people do sitting behind a desk, and that 'teaching' is essentially about explaining things and setting exercises to ensure comprehension.[17] Plainly, you cannot develop the creativity of children and young people without an approach that views teaching as rather more of a creative process than these young people had experienced.

Creativity may be within all our capabilities, but it doesn't happen in a vacuum. Just as children and young people need a climate that supports their creative efforts, adults also need a climate conducive to stimulating their own creative capacity: a working atmosphere marked by openness, acceptance of difference, with a positive attitude to new ideas – what has been called a 'congenial' environment.[18]

But of course, a climate conducive to stimulating creativity doesn't just happen. It depends upon the application of insight and skills: two aptitudes that were unfortunately sadly lacking in Paul (see Missed Opportunity). As you'll see in the next section, the process of establishing such a working environment can be is just as much a demonstration of creativity as other more overt activities.

CREATIVE LEADERSHIP THINKING SPACE

- To what degree would you say your working environment is a 'congenial' environment for stimulating creative capacity?

- How might you encourage 'openness, acceptance of difference, a positive attitude to new ideas'?

Creativity is ... not restricted to certain activities

The rapid social, economic and technological changes we are experiencing are placing different requirements upon organisations, and upon individuals. Consequently, we need to understand creativity as something no longer limited to artistic endeavour, nor restricted to innovative product development in the corporate world. We need to 'chunk up' from artistic and practical activities to envisage creativity as an over-arching human attribute.

One way of moving from a narrow interpretation of creativity has been to refer to the sort of exceptional creativity that occurs in the arts and sciences as 'high creativity'. As we are all increasingly required to be more 'self-directed', Anna Craft and her colleagues suggest that the qualities associated with self-direction (or put another way personal agency) might be termed 'little c creativity':

> 'Little c creativity'[ ] focuses on the resourcefulness and agency of ordinary people, rather than the extraordinary contributions and insights of the few. It has to do with a 'can-do' attitude to 'real life' ...[19]

Thinking about it this way, 'little c' creativity can be described as a sort of 'personal effectiveness'; an attitude of life that is driven by 'possibility thinking', about acting effectively with flexibility and novelty in the everyday rather than the extraordinary.[20]

It then follows, as Sir Ken Robinson puts it, that:

'Scientists, technologists, business people, educators, anyone can be creative in the work they do. Creativity is not exclusive to particular activities; it's possible wherever human intelligence is actively engaged. It is not a specific type of activity but a quality of intelligence'.[21]

Of course for educators, there is a dual aspect. Leaders need to develop a creative workforce – teachers who are able to engage students by teaching creatively, using imaginative approaches to make learning interesting, avoiding the mind-numbing features described in the example from the MORI research earlier. In addition, teaching *for* creativity must also extend to the nurture of 'little c creativity' in young people. As Anna Craft describes it, this will be about encouraging children and young people to pose questions, identify problems for themselves, placing ownership and control over the learning process with the learner.[22]

Creative teaching may also involve teaching *for* creativity, but it may not always be the case. You may have experienced the dynamic, imaginative teacher who holds their class spellbound, but whose style depends upon their own strong personality, rather than focusing on developing the personal agency of young people. Anna Craft concludes that creative teaching may, but does not necessarily, lead to learner creativity. But teaching *for* creativity is as much a demonstration of a teacher's creativity as creative teaching:

'A pedagogy which fosters creativity depends on practitioners being creative to provide the ethos for enabling children's creativity; in other words, one that is relevant to them and in which they can take ownership of the knowledge, skills and understanding to be learnt'.[23]

There is, of course, the issue of how values influence the different creative styles. Organisational and personal values influence behaviour, and the values of a dynamic, charismatic performer may be different from the values of the practitioner who adopts an open and inclusive style. More about values later, but while we've been considering classroom teaching, there is also an application to leadership. A strong, charismatic leader may be creative and original and their style will emanate from certain values. The values will be very different when leadership takes the form of leadership *for* creativity: because in this case their personal contribution may lie in the role of what

Arthur Cropley has called creativity 'assisters' – people who can energise, activate and release creativity in others without necessarily producing novelty themselves.[24] They will be people who can stimulate a 'congenial' working environment, whose strength lies in nurturing the confidence, capabilities and creativity of others. Yet if we take 'little c creativity' to mean the personal effectiveness that facilitates new and productive outcomes, it is just as much a demonstration of creativity to inspire others to develop in their own way. Both for individual development, and for productive team working, the skills and attributes of 'assisters' can make a significant impact.

> 'People need confidence in themselves to energise others. Some people naturally have that ability'
>
> Paul, consultant on complexity theory and leadership
>
> 'My first Principal was an inspiration. It was her that gave me the final courage and inspiration to become a Principal myself'.
>
> Dick, Principal of a Further Education College
>
> 'I've known a lot of late bloomers who've been encouraged to recognize their talents. It needs recognition, nurture and develop, then off you go.'
>
> Janet, Primary School teacher

Creativity as a process

Having considered what creativity is 'not' plainly it's helpful to try to define some features of creativity. We've seen that there is the 'thinking' part of being able to think about things differently, of having a solution-focus, a 'can-do' attitude. And there is also the 'doing' part: behaviours that create new realities, or that enable others to develop their own personal effectiveness. 'Innovation' has been used as the more relevant term for describing corporate exploitation of new ideas into profitable outcomes. The outcomes of education are much more complex, and can be less tangible depending upon the view you take of the purpose of education. Therefore 'creative' can be a more appropriate term to encompass the multiplicity of outcomes of educational leadership.

It's because of this complexity that the 'doing' part of creativity in education will occur in many forms. It may range from the example of Michael

Wilshaw in establishing a whole institution as his 'personal creation', to a team leader with the skills and attitude to facilitate the personal development of colleagues, and of course will include establishing an ethos and practice of 'teaching *for* creativity'. So thinking about creativity as a *process* can help us to recognise that creativity can be as multi-faceted as the range of human ingenuity.

Despite the difference between education and the corporate world, there are still things we can learn from research into the role of creativity in innovative product development. Interestingly, when Michael Mumford and his colleagues looked at this, they found that leadership was conspicuously absent from the list of potential influences. They point out that, traditionally, leadership has not been held to be a particularly significant influence on creativity and innovation, and therefore leadership may have been discounted in this respect.[25]

But of course in education we've moved on from that position. If educators are being called to stimulate creativity in children and young people, then plainly they will need to be involved in creative work themselves, and this has to start with leadership.

So while Michael and his colleagues looked at influences on creativity in relation to the development of ideas into useful products, for our purposes, we can see how their analysis might apply in an educational setting. If we look first at the features that the research suggests are integral to creative work, we can then map those features against a 'real-life' illustration of creative leadership.

First, creative work involves *defining a problem, gathering information,* then progressively refining and extending initial ideas to a successful conclusion. Because this may be a difficult process, creative work can be expected to be *demanding and time consuming.* This being the case, there's an implication that *high levels of motivation* may be needed. Then from an organizational point of view, different groups of people may devote time and effort, there may need to be an investment of other resources, so that creative work may be *resource intensive.* Given this, *persuasion and politics* are likely to play a role.

As creativity is an iterative process which may generate multiple solutions, creative work can also be *uncertain.* Because uncertainty can go hand in hand with risk, most creative work will involve *risky ventures.* Part of that risk will stem from the need to experiment and to be able to *tolerate failure.* Finally, Michael and his colleagues point to an important factor that is often overlooked: the fact that the success of creative work will depend upon it being *contextualised.*[26]

As far as education is concerned, the issue of context is indeed crucial to creative work, as you will see from the next chapter. But it's also useful to consider how the features that Michael and his colleagues identified stand up against an example of work in education. **Leading a creative project** describes how Faculty Head Denise melded the elements to create a course that won many awards, including the 'Oscar' of UK colleges, the Beacon Award.

Leading a creative project

Denise is a Faculty Head at a further education college. One of her strengths is her ability to network: she had built up a range of both public sector and business contacts, mainly with the purpose of seeking valuable work experience opportunities for her students. Denise had noticed that the issue of young people who had become disengaged was attracting political attention at a national level to the degree that they had acquired their own label (NEETs – not in education, employment or training). But she became aware that the dilemma of these young people was also a local issue when it began to be discussed with some passion at meetings she attended. This was when she posed the question 'Why isn't my college doing something about this?'

So Denise took the initiative in linking with the workers who were in direct contact with young people falling into this category. Debbie, the local authority manager for 'looked-after children', Simon the achievement leader for the local youth services, and Mark, who's role was to co-ordinate local services for young people falling into the category of NEET.

The first thing these contacts told Denise was that what the college currently had to offer was of no use to these young people. As most of them had dropped out of school at age 12 or 13, most had not attained an academic standard to make them eligible for even the most basic courses. Apart from the academic element, the college was not accessible enough for young people with considerable additional needs, who were unlikely to attend college on a regular basis without a network of support (*defining the problem*).

Realising that a bespoke course would be needed, Denise invited one of her most creative lecturers to come up with course design ideas for pre-entry level students. This was a completely new area for the college, and Denise began to realise the potential issues (*uncertain*). To cover the practical arrangements, she consulted with relevant people in the college, both to seek their advice, and to get them on board with the idea: Mike the estates manager for appropriate room allocation, Jan the learning resources manager, and the in-house student support workers. In the background for some of these young people were issues such as gun and knife crime, drug and alcohol addiction, so the college needed to take a careful risk assessment (*risky ventures*). The third strand of this phase was to link up with social workers and learning coaches already in touch with the young people to tease out how a framework of practical support could work (*gathering information*).

Up to this stage, a lot of people had given their time to the process (*demanding and time-consuming*). While the project had begun because Denise had been caught up with the advocacy of others on behalf of these young people, it needed her ability to pass on and sustain that enthusiasm to keep others on board (*high levels of motivation*).

The final course was the result of a year of planning and consultation. During this time, Denise made sure she gained the support of the Senior Management Team, and also the Board of Governors at the college (*persuasion and politics*).

The aim to re-engage, educate and certificate hard to reach young people meant that the course design had particular features. In order to have maximum impact, it was delivered over five days, as against the three day delivery of most college courses, and extended over 48 weeks, unlike the 35 weeks in the remainder of the college (*resource intensive*). A 'roll on roll off' enrolment between September and March meant that young people could commence the course as soon as they were identified. The expected outcome was to support learners to achieve nine qualifications which would enable them to progress to either Level 1 programmes in the college, to enter work-based learning or employment.

During the first run of the course, 42 learners were enrolled. There were six non-starters, six withdrew from the course, and two were excluded (*tolerate failure*). On the upside, seven learners were successfully moved up one or more levels due to their ability. For the rest of the learners, both attainment and progression were predicted at 100 per cent.

The outcome was an award-winning course. Both in the initial generation of the idea and its development and implementation, it took account of all the relevant factors in the local context (*contextualised*). Indeed, as you will see in the next chapter, context is a crucial consideration in creative leadership.

Creativity as democratic practice

Denise's NEETs project highlights a third aspect of the application of creativity in education. Successive governments and policy makers have sought to use standardization as the main thrust of policy in striving to raise achievement. In the UK from the imposition of the National Curriculum in 1988, government policy has crossed the school gate and sought to dictate *how* teachers teach and well as *what* they teach. In the US in 2002 the 'No Child Left Behind' Act specified how often states were to test children, what subjects were to be emphasized, and how much progress should be made in a year for every subject.

Underpinning these initiatives has been the laudable goals of raising achievement overall and reducing the achievement gap between the highest and lowest achieving young people. Yet despite the worthy aims, the gap has not been reduced to a level of parity of achievement for all young people. In the US, a report in 2009 warned that, on average, Black and Latino students were roughly two to three years of learning behind White students of the same age. In the UK, for the vast majority of white working-class students and some ethnic minorities the achievement gap remains unacceptably wide, and on current rates of improvement will take decades before there is any sense of parity.[27]

The conclusion is stark, and has been succinctly summed up by headteacher of Phoenix High School, Sir William Atkinson:

'...although central government can set a framework, determine structure, have a national vision, set targets, provide funding, provide teaching and non-teaching staff in school and support the development of links between schools and external entities, ultimately, they are unable to reach down and determine standards achieved by little Johnny in school X in Newport.'[28]

Sir William was speaking in Wales, which accounts for the reference to a school in Newport. But you could replace that with reference to any school in any town in the land. But the point is well made that, despite worthy efforts by governments, it is what happens in the classroom that is the difference that makes a difference. It is the creative response to local issues by teachers and leaders that will ultimately resolve the issue of ensuring parity of achievement for all children and young people. Attempting to standardize or replicate particular ways of working across the complexity of social and educational environments does not necessarily encourage adaptability and responsiveness to local situations. The emergence of a centralised pedagogy (or 'one best way' approach to lesson delivery) potentially diminishes the 'creative space' within which teachers can exercise professional judgement.[29]

As you will see in the next chapter, all leadership operates in a particular environment. In acknowledging the achievement gap we are drawn to the conclusion that standardisation and adopting 'one best way' have not ensured parity for all students. Rather it is the *response-ability* of leaders and teachers that is the more relevant factor. In this respect, creative responses to local environments can define creativity as a democratic practice.

The challenge

This chapter has defined creativity on a very broad canvas. Creativity has been described not as a single entity, something that some people have and others do not. Rather it is seen as ability we have all been born with, a function of intelligence that takes many forms. It is not limited to certain activities, but can be demonstrated across all aspects of human endeavour. The notion of 'little c creativity' has been used to acknowledge everyday individual resourcefulness as a demonstration of creativity.

Even so, there are aspects of our modern life – particularly in relation to education – that prevail against the expression of individual creativity, and thus it needs to be fostered. Children and young people need a climate that encourages their creative capacity, and adults also need a congenial working environment and the opportunities to demonstrate their creativity. Thus, having recognized the universal nature of creativity, the challenge for a creative leader is to turn problems to opportunities by stimulating an educational environment that enables all to develop their creative capacity.

CREATIVE LEADERSHIP THINKING SPACE

This chapter has described features of creative work revealed by research, and mapped them against an educational project in order to identify the success factors. Learning can also be gained by using the method to identify deficiencies in the case of a creative project that may not have been as successful. So taking an example of an initiative from your own experience, think about how each of these elements were featured, and whether any elements that might be missing could have contributed to a more successful outcome:

- How was the problem recognised and defined? What information gathering was needed?
- How were the time demands managed?
- What degree of motivation was needed to maintain the project?
- How were additional resources obtained?
- Was persuasion and political influence needed? How was it achieved?
- How did you and others deal with uncertainty?
- How was risk managed?
- Was there a tolerance of failure?
- How was the project relevant to its context?
- Can you identify features that define creativity as democratic practice?

Notes

1 John Adair 2009:118
2 Robert Sternberg 2005:349
3 See Feldman et al. 1994
4 As described by Anna Craft et al. 2001:48
5 Mark Runco 2004:21
6 Tim Smit, Foreword to Anna Craft 2005:xivf
7 Phil Beadle 2010:3–61
8 Peter Wilby, *The Guardian,* 5 January 2010
9 Roland Bel 2010:47
10 http://www.adb.org/documents/information/knowledge-solutions/
   harnessing-creativity-and-innovation-in-the-workplace.pdf accessed 4
   September 2011
11 Peter Wilby, *The Guardian,* 5 January 2010
12 Robert Fisher 2005:28
13 Sir Ken Robinson 2001:111
14 Guy Claxton 2008:22
15 Robert Fisher 2005:27
16 Anna Craft 1999:137
17 Guy Claxton 2008:72
18 Mihayli Csikszentmihalyi 1996
19 Anna Craft et al. 2001:49
20 Anna Craft 2002:43
21 Sir Ken Robinson 2001:113
22 Anna Craft 2005:42
23 *Ibid.* 2005:44
24 Arthur J. Cropley 2001:67
25 Michael Mumford et al. 2002:705–50
26 Ibid. 2002:709
27 Sir William Atkinson 2009
28 *Ibid.* 2009:7
29 Pamela Burnard and June White 2008:669

PART II

The Practice: Inspire, Motivate, Grow

6

The Context: Creating the Environment for Creativity

This chapter will be proposing the environment as a key influential factor in leadership as creativity. It is how a leader responds and adapts to their environment that defines their leadership as creative. Each educational environment will be different; the variables are so numerous that it would seem impossible to find a definitive model of leadership to fit all contexts. However, this chapter will suggest a framework of Inspire – Motivate – Grow for use as a template for understanding the characteristics of Leadership as Creativity

When I taught in school, there was a colleague who had a particular gripe. It was something she returned to time and time again. Whenever there was a issue or problem with the behaviour of students, you could rely on her to come out with it. 'Ah well' she would pronounce sagely 'if only we had carpets in the school, the behaviour would be better'. Accompanied by a look that was suggesting 'I told you so', this was her single answer to any behavioural problem.

At one level I suppose she was probably right. Sociologists would tell us that physical environment will indeed influence people's behaviour. So carpeting the corridors and classrooms at my school may have had an impact on the behaviour of the students. But perhaps only in the short term, because the physical environment is only one aspect of the context in which we work.

The context is indeed complex and multi-faceted. The people around us and their behaviour are part of it; the professional environment in which work makes a contribution, as do the values and beliefs of the establishment in which we spend our time. They contribute – or otherwise – to an environment for creativity.

Then again, we all work in different contexts at the same time. Like the ripples from dropping a pebble into a pool, they spread out around us, generating their particular influence. A teacher will work in the context of their classroom, but also in the context of their department and their school, which includes the context of the board of governors and of the management team. Then there are the contexts of the teaching profession, the local community, and the education system as a whole.

All the contexts we inhabit exert an influence on us, and of course the influence is two-way. Teachers are a particular environmental influence upon children and young people, and leaders are an environmental influence on everyone they come into contact with. In fact, as Neil Dempster has put it succinctly:

'Leadership is not a phenomenon that has any real meaning until it is attached to a particular context'.[1]

CREATIVE LEADERSHIP THINKING SPACE

- Thinking about the *context* of your creative leadership – where and how is it evident and visible?

- Where is it visible, in the classrooms, in the corridors?

The power of environmental influence

Trying to assess the degree of influence of an environmental factor is an intriguing issue.

It's a tantalising question whether teachers actually make a difference, or whether the combined forces of genetics and social environment have power to override the effects of teaching, however well intentioned. The nature versus nurture debate swings from the view of geneticists who have claimed cleverness is something we inherit – which raises the question of why bother educating – to the position that social environment and experiences have more influence over young people's potential and capability.

At the height of the debate, the study of identical twins separated at birth and reared in different environments was thought an ideal subject to cast light on the comparative influence of genetics and environment. The work of Janet Taylor and her colleagues at Florida State University is some of the latest in a proliferation of research, this time focusing on comparing reading ability in identical and non-identical twins. Since identical twins share 100 per cent of their genes while fraternal twins only 50 per cent, if a trait was genetic, it could be expected that identical twins would share more similarity in that respect than non-identical twins. But if a trait was entirely environmental, it could be expected that identical twins would share or differ in that feature to the same extent as other twins.

What made this study of particular interest was that, in focusing on reading ability, they also assessed the teachers. By examining the grade averages for all the children in each teacher's class, they assessed teacher quality by how much the grade averages improved over a year. Of course there are many other variables that could be taken into account when trying to assess whether a particular effect is due to environment – factors such as socio-economic group or family support. This study only examined the results of the teaching of reading.

In focusing on the twins in each class, the team found that the difference in reading ability between identical and non-identical twins was greatest in the classes with good teachers. But when less effective teachers were at the front of the class, the differences were less evident. Their conclusion was that in those classes where children did less well, it was environment rather than genes that had the biggest impact on performance. In other words, the suggestion is that good teachers are able to get the best from their students, but less able teachers allow children's backgrounds to affect their performance.[2]

Good teachers, as an environmental influence, make a difference.

Response-ability

Janet Taylor's research is not the only illustration that what happens in the classroom makes a difference. Pam Sammons and her colleagues have also shown that the influence of overall teaching quality on reading and mathematics has been stronger than the net influence of some background factors, including being eligible for free school meals.[3]

This book has not been concerned specifically with aspects of pedagogy, rather with how leaders stimulate creativity. But the point we can take from the results of the research is to recognise that we work in a particular context, and that we are an environmental factor that exerts an influence on the people we come into contact with. Accepting that teachers are an environmental influence that can override social and genetic factors plainly means we need to be highly tuned to how we use that influence.

What good teachers and leaders do, of course, is adjust their behaviour according to the context in which they are working. Just as teachers adjust their teaching strategies to match the learning level of their students, effective leaders adapt their behaviour depending upon the context in which they are operating. To do this they have to be able to 'read' people, situations and circumstances, they have to practice 'context-sensitivity'. It's an ability that relies on a number of personal attributes, not least of which are the abilities to be approachable, open-minded and flexible.[4]

In Chapter 5 the example of Denise's work to create a bespoke course for young people who were NEET was an illustration of a creative response that involved working across several contexts. Denise became aware that the issue of NEETs was causing concern in a political context, and she linked into the context of the local community to develop a response. She then had to work in the context of her team of lecturers to construct a course, and won support from a whole-college context including the context of the board of governors. Many of the features of Denise's approach are mirrored in the work of Ephraim Weisstein in the US (see *Schools for the Future*) which is also a response to a national issue that involved working creatively at college level.

CREATIVE LEADERSHIP THINKING SPACE

Do you have an example of your own where you've made links between different events in different contexts to come up with a creative initiative?

Schools for the Future

Ephraim Weisstein is a consultant best known for inventing Diploma Plus, a nationally acclaimed alternative high school model operating in 30 schools in eight states of the US and serving 4,000 formerly disconnected youth. Ephraim asserts that many existing structures of schooling no longer make sense (if they ever did). For instance, 'advancement toward graduation by time in seat'. Rather, Ephraim advocates a strategy of 'If they learn quick – move them on. If they need more time – allow for it'. Some food for thought there as regards the UK system, e.g. what would it look like if the process of education was focused on the learning needs of the young person, rather than fitting the young person to the system?

Ephraim describes the Schools for the Future model being launched in the state of Massachusetts in 2011 as a 'New High School Model for Struggling Youth'. The aim is to provide innovative educational provision for young people who are behind academically or disengaged from education altogether. In order to meet the needs of high-risk youth, the model is conceived as 'learning-recovery-and-accelerator-in-one', with an aim of achieving an average of 2 years academic gain for every 1 year in the program. Certain core principles underpin the design of the model:

- **Individual personal development is crucial to learning progression**. The emphasis is on stimulating self-efficacy, social and emotional literacy and developing problem-solving in small groups. Activities are designed to inspire a 'can-do' spirit and help students produce work of which they can be proud. Students gain the mental framework they need to be strong readers, mathematicians, thinkers and learners.
- **Individual pathways mean progression is based on individual student achievement rather than any other factor such as age**. If students need more time at one stage they get it. Progression also applies to the design of the activities. As students gain confidence and skills, they gain more independence. They advance from a tight programme where English and Maths are seen as the building blocks and integrated across all subjects, to independent project work driven by their own interests and aided by technology that drives student engagement.
- **Technology is a lever that drives student engagement.** A 'blended etech platform' provides instructional and professional development support on-demand to encourage anytime/anywhere learning. An extensive electronic virtual campus can extend learning by as much as 50 per cent beyond the traditional school year.

Adaptability

One of the core principles of Diploma Plus is that students have an individualised learning pathway. Indeed there have been government initiatives in

UK and US with similar worthy aims. Yet as you will have seen previously in this book, the systemic force of standardisation of schooling has served to dampen rather than heighten the potential of all young people to achieve their individual potential. Even when the aim of policy is to raise individual achievement, there is still the perception that a uniform approach will achieve this.

The standardisation of teaching has been seen as a key area for policy makers to influence raising achievement. The terms 'good', 'best' and 'excellent' practice have been bandied around, sometimes used inter-changeably. And yet, there appears to be little attempt to define the difference between them. Frank Coffield and Sheila Edward have challenged the rhetoric that has applied the terms to the further education sector in a drive to raise standards.[5] They suggest that 'excellent' practice must be a more broad-based term, since excellent practices flourish in many colleges, just as there are plenty of excellent football teams in the Premier League but only one 'best' team. But they challenge how the 'Champion of the Agenda for Change' at the Learning and Skills Council can claim that he has been 'looking at best practice and publicising it':

> '...how does he know that what he looks at *is* best practice? What criteria or norms is he using to make these judgements? How does he deal with the immense diversity and complexity of local contexts? Will best practice be used by other tutors just because it has been so labelled and publicised? And what are the implications for the quality of teaching and learning in colleges if he is wrong?'[6]

Given the vast range of educational contexts it's plainly not helpful to attempt to standardize 'best' practice, since what works well in one context may need significant adaptation to be effective in another. Indeed, as Coffield and Edward point out, a notion of a single 'best' solution to a wide range of complex problems has also been seen by some commentators as the beginning of the slide into authoritarianism.[7]

In practice, it makes no sense to suggest that the practice of teaching should not differ depending upon the educational context. Effective teachers will have a lesson plan, but even the same lesson will be subtly different each time they experience it. They will modify and adjust their behaviour (and even the plan) in order to maximise their students' learning. Similarly, effective leaders will have an overall objective. To achieve it, most successful leaders have learned to behave differently in different places at different times.[8]

Saying that teaching and leadership will differ according to the context is not the same as saying there should not be the similarly high aims in relation to outcomes despite different contexts. Rather, to attempt to standardize the *process* of achieving those aims is to ignore the level of adaptability needed to match the approach to the context.

> '*My approach is the same now as six years ago – but six years ago it wasn't working. The team respond now. The style I was using was inappropriate for the context and I didn't have the ability to adjust my style'.*
>
> Gordon – Research and Consultancy Director

CREATIVE LEADERSHIP THINKING SPACE

How well do you adapt your behaviour to different contexts, different people?

Culture as an environmental influence

Put most simply, culture can be described as 'the way we do things round here'; John West-Burnham describes it as encompassing the language, symbolism and behaviours of an organization.[9] There will be long-established and deep, embedded ground rules, habits of thinking and acting that govern the way an organisation operates. The message may be subtle because it is conveyed through language and rituals that are taken for granted. But the overall effect is powerful. The way people talk and act is the crucial channel for conveying the values of the organisation.

The experience of merging institutions can throw into sharp relief the importance of culture as an environmental influence. It's been a recent experience for many educators in the UK that they've been required to manage the merging of institutions. Whether as a response to falling rolls, or in the interests of efficiency and effectiveness, educators have had to negotiate the merging of nursery and primary schools, or on a larger scale, the combining of further education colleges or universities into single institutions.

The practical issues of merging can be immense. Not surprisingly, the bigger the institutions, the bigger the issues. Consensus has to be achieved in respect of a whole raft of policies, governance and management structures, IT functions, telephone systems, etc. Agreement has to be reached on a new name and logo, branding and signage. Lack of consensus or agreement can delay the process, or even derail it.

At a practical level, there is much to be learned from mergers that have already taken place. However, there is one important aspect that is frequently overlooked. The urgency of the practical issues to be decided often distract from tackling an important issue with both short and long-term implications: that of merging two different cultures.

Where the merger is more of a 'takeover', with a larger institution absorbing a lesser one, perhaps the assumption may be made that the culture of the larger will automatically subsume that of the lesser. Which would be a flawed assumption: people cling on to their ways of doing things, and without time and effort devoted to evolving a new and original ethos, two separate sub-cultures will inevitably trundle on, harming the overall effectiveness of the organisation.

To be effective, the work towards a cultural change needs to occur at different levels. College Principal Dick was telling me how this was brought about when his college took over a failing school. He arranged meetings with parents, giving them feedback. He spent time explaining the vision of transformation into a technology-based school with the best equipment. The introduction of a uniform made a difference because it distinguished the re-formed school from the previous one. The overall aim was to make the school proud of itself. Creating a new confidence led to better behaviour, which was better for the teachers. Significantly, the cultural change could be evidenced in the staff sickness rate, which went from 260 days to just 12 in the first term.

Even where mergers are a marriage of more or less equal partners, the issue of differing cultures still has to be addressed. Imagine a hypothetical example of two colleges of fairly equal size and learning achievements. College A retains a fairly traditional hierarchical management structure. The Principal and senior executives take decisions, which are then passed down to department heads as instructions for implementation. Compliance and consistency are seen as beneficial, and the procedures and ways of working are the same throughout the college.

College B has developed a consensual management style. The Principal and senior executives discuss options with the department heads, who are encouraged to make a case for how they would like to run things in their department. There is a degree of freedom to experiment: if a proposal is considered to have value, managers are encouraged to take forward their own initiatives.

This is not to say that one style is good and another not so good. Taken to extreme, either style can prove problematic. An autocratic leadership with excessive insistence on compliance can dampen enthusiasm and stifle creativity. On the other hand, leaders need to be decisive, it's their role after all to lead and give direction. And an overly consensual climate can delay decision-making to the extent of being a source of frustration for staff needing direction.

The point being made here is that the culture of an organization is as much a contextual influence as the physical environment. Differing cultures as outlined above will not be evident from organizational charts. Yet the effect of attempting to merge different cultures can be significant and generate disagreements and misunderstanding. In this respect the phrase ' a multitude of truths' is an apt summing up of the complexities of merging cultures.[10] It needs time spent in peeling back the layers of practice and ritual to achieve a new consensus on the style and purpose of a single organisation.

(Talking about mergers) *'There can be an assumption that people will fit in with people. Yet different reactions can be cultural reactions. You need to assess the culture to predict how parts of the organization will react. Early on you need to talk about and identify the desired culture and work out the transitional steps you'll need'.*

Gordon – Research & Consultancy Director

A mismatch can also occur at an individual level, as when a person takes up a new post and misjudges the organizational culture. This can occur when transferring to a different department within a single organi- sation, because departments can have their own unique 'sub-culture'. Or it can be when moving to a different organisation, as Robert Sternberg has described. In this example, a superintendent moved from a large urban district in the Eastern US to a comparable urban district in the Western US. The districts were comparable in size, yet the cultures of the school districts and local environment were very different. One district had a small minority population, the other a large one; one district had power concentrated in a small number of people, the other had a more diffused and informal structure. This superintendent lasted little more than a year in his new post, mainly because he went into the job all fired up with what he *thought* needed to be done, with no attempt to judge the prevailing, and very different, culture:

'His vision and method of implementation did not fit into the new culture, and he did not take the time to listen and learn so that he could have adapted his vision to the new community he was serving. His leadership thus failed.'[11]

A culture for learning 1 – The Foundation Stage in Wales

Becoming fully operational in 2011, the Foundation Phase introduced by the Welsh Government is a creative initiative designed to meet the developmental needs of young children. In practical terms, it combined Early Years Education (for 3 to 5-year-olds) and Key Stage 1 (5 to 7-year-olds) of the National Curriculum. It built on research that showed children do not begin to benefit from formal teaching until the age of six or seven, and incorporated features of Scandinavian 'forest schools'.

The emphasis is on learning by doing and active involvement with a curriculum that covers personal, social, emotional, physical and intellectual well-being so as to develop the whole child. It places great importance on children using the outdoors to experiment, explore and take risks. The aim is to encourage the development of creative, expressive and observational skills, and nurture positive attitudes to learning so that children enjoy it and want to continue.

Overall, an initial evaluation of the Foundation Phase by the Welsh inspectorate Estyn found the impact on the well-being of children had been positive. In particular, active learning approaches and the use of the outdoor learning environment were helping boys to be more engaged in their learning. Yet in a minority of schools this was not the case, because leaders and practitioners did not understand the principles and practice of the Foundation Phase. In a few schools, leaders were not convinced about the educational value of the Foundation Phase or did not know enough about it to ensure that it was implemented effectively.[12]

The environment for learning

The Foundation Phase (see *A culture for learning 1*) is an interesting illustration of how the environment for learning has changed. The past educational culture that constrained learning within the four walls of a classroom has gradually shifted to allow children and young people to support their academic learning from wider experiences. Plainly the opportunities that children have for rich and varied experiences outside schooling differ according to their social circumstances. So it is encouraging that the Foundation Phase offers the opportunity for even the youngest children to enjoy exploration in a garden or woodland environment that might otherwise not be available to them. It's encouraging also, that the report of the inspectorate highlights the fact that the use of the outdoor environment and the active learning approaches are helping boys to be more involved in their learning.

Of course, as we've been including culture as part of the environmental influences, there's a relevant point in the report in the reference to a minority of leaders and practitioners not understanding the principles and practice of the Foundation Phase, and further, not being convinced of its education value. Perhaps some might say this was an indication of a lack of investment in training. But you could also speculate that the subtle yet pervasive influence of local culture might have a role to play.

The 'stickiness' of 'the way we do things round here' can prove a factor that delays the take-up of new policy initiatives. 'Cultural lag' is a phrase used by sociologists to describe the slowness of one part of a culture to keep pace with another, particularly the gap between material inventions and their take-up in society. It's often quoted that there was 50 years between the invention of the typewriter and its widespread use in society. Arguably, that particular gap may not be as evident with our current fast pace of developing technology. But the idea of 'cultural lag' can still be in evidence in the gap between policy initiatives and their take-up in practice.

It's possible that the reported lack of conviction of some leaders in the educational value of the Foundation Phase is due in part to a cultural 'resistance'. It's an illustration that the effective take-up of new central policies or even new local initiatives cannot merely be assumed. Local culture plays a part in the readiness – or otherwise – to adopt new ways of doing things. An 'environment for learning' can refer to a leaders' role in creating an educational context that supports and encourages student learning. But it also encompasses a cultural ethos that stimulates *everyone* to engage in their own personal and professional learning and development.

A culture for learning 2 – Developing emotional literacy

A creative initiative often comes about when a leader is able to make an original link between seemingly different events or information. So it was when Siriol was inspired to set up a project to nurture emotional literacy at Welsh-medium secondary school Ysgol Plasmawr. The first seed was planted in Siriol's mind as a result of a debate amongst the senior management team about the sort of school they wanted Ysgol Plasmawr to be. The second link came from the results of a student questionnaire used to tease out issues of student well-being. In response to one of the questions – 'Who would you be most likely to tell if you were being bullied?' – the vast majority of students opted for 'A friend'. The third and final link came when Siriol went on a course on motivational interviewing. Impressed with Karen the trainer, things clicked together for Siriol: if students would prefer to talk to a friend about issues such as bullying, why didn't they train them in skills of motivational interviewing to enable them to be peer mentors and counsellors?

With Siriol's enthusiasm to drive it forward, the project became an exemplar for a pastoral initiative that enabled young people to become more grounded human beings by having had emotional support. Following training, the young volunteers took up roles as either peer mentors focusing on academic mentoring, or peer counsellors providing emotional support for issues such as bullying. Both the training and the roles were seen as enhancing emotional literacy through the development of leadership skills. Mentors could meet up with younger pupils through the school's system of vertical registration, and they also offered help at breaks and lunchtimes. Similarly, peer counsellors also made themselves available during breaks.

The training in communication generally was extended out to families, with Karen running workshops for parents on communication with young people on issues such as substance misuse. And the theme of developing emotional literacy was extended to practice in other areas of leadership skills for students. Junior sports leaders were coaching younger pupils, and also began coaching in local primary schools. Yet a further development focused on raising self-esteem for girls.

With such a strong emphasis on pastoral support, I raised a question with Siriol on whether there was any evidence that this support impacted upon education attainment? A difficult question to answer given the range of variables affecting attainment. Siriol pointed first to the social mix of the school, with 30 per cent of their intake being drawn from areas of social deprivation. Yet examination results appeared to be better than might be expected according to value added criteria, with 73 per cent of pupils achieving A*-C at GCSE. Also of significance was the fact that the school had the lowest exclusion rate in the county.

But the project was not all about achievement in examinations: it was about creating a culture within which young people could develop their emotional literacy and boost their self-confidence and self-esteem. It was contributing to an holistic educational experience for the young people involved.

There are two aspects of relevance to an environment for learning in the example in *A Culture for Learning 2*. First, Siriol did not only bring in Karen, a professional trainer, to train the students. She asked her to train the teachers as well. A whole school involvement was crucial to ensure students had the support of teachers in facilitating the practical arrangements. Training the teachers smoothed the way for staff to 'buy into' the initiative right from the start. Karen's professional skills enabled her to adjust her approach to counter any resistance that arose, and generally stimulate engagement in the project. (It's interesting that Karen found the response of the young people very refreshing: they didn't display the entrenched viewpoints sometimes found in adults, but openly accepted difference in other young people).

The second point illustrates how there can sometimes be barriers to the take-up of even worthwhile initiatives with proven benefit. There had been a lot of local interest, both generally in the high profile given to the pastoral element at Ysgol Plasmawr, and specifically in the project of developing students as peer mentors and counsellors. Yet despite widespread acceptance that it was a project that benefitted the culture of the school as well as the individual students, many teachers had commented to Siriol that 'it could never happen in our school'.[13]

There could be many factors that might account for this: another school might feel it would be a distraction from a strong focus on academic achievement; there might be an attitude of 'teacher as authority figure' that would not sit well with empowering students to act as mentors and counsellors; there could be a lack of openness to the learning required to broaden teachers experience from subject specialists to take a more holistic educational role in developing emotional literacy. All these aspects are cultural features that can impact upon whether or not there will be a successful take-up of creative initiatives. Even when a project is recognized as being innovative and beneficial for students, the cultural barriers of wider dissemination cannot be underestimated.

CREATIVE LEADERSHIP THINKING SPACE

How are you role-modelling creative leadership for young people and teachers?

The context for leadership as creativity

The majority of past psychological research on creativity has concentrated on the thought processes, emotions, and motivations of individuals who produce novelty: the 'creative personality'. However, more recently, it has become increasingly clear that we need to consider the variables external to the individual if we want to explain why, when, and from where new ideas arise.[14] You cannot understand creativity in an individual, say a leader, without taking account of the context.

The point was made in Chapter 5 that, despite the laudable goals of governments in the UK and US, the gap between the highest and lowest achieving young people has not been reduced to a level of parity for all young people.

Headteacher Sir William Atkinson outlined the problem in his 2009 Wales Education Lecture. He went on to suggest we could take an example from any cookbook written by a leading chef to understand why the achievement in the education system is still so variable. Using a complicated recipe for Thai Green Curry (some 24 ingredients), he questioned why, despite having all the basic ingredients, his efforts in producing the dish invariably fell short of perfection:

> 'Success has something to do with the quality of the ingredients used throughout and the preparation and skill in blending all the elements into a successful meal possessing the desired flavours and accents.'[15]

For a leader to demonstrate creativity, the 'skill in blending all the elements' will need to include adaptability and response-ability to the context and environment – that of the classroom, of the school, of the local community. As the quote from Neil Dempster earlier in this chapter suggested, leadership has no real meaning until it is attached to a particular context. Therefore, the framework presented in the diagram below represents key personal elements of a leader functioning within a context. It is a symbiotic relationship within which the environment impacts upon leadership, and a leader influences the environment by means of key elements of leadership: here defined as Vision and Values, Relationships and Personal Attributes.

A framework for leadership as creativity: Inspire – Motivate – Grow (IMG)

I've also stated previously that this book will not contain a definitive model for creative leadership. The variables are so many and complex I don't believe it would be possible to do that. Robert Sternberg has also claimed that there is probably no model of leadership that will totally capture all the many facts – internal and external to the individual – that make for a successful leader.[16] However, as the diagram indicates, there are some key factors that can be captured under the broad headings of the following chapters:

Inspire, Motivate, Grow (IMG) are not definitive descriptors. Rather, they serve as headings under which to cluster the differing variables and characteristics of leadership in particular contexts. IMG is also an indicator of the differences between leadership and management. It serves as a guide to the step change from managerialist concerns with procedures, systems and efficiency, where the view of the context is as fixed and stable. It allows us to use a pathway of processes and effectiveness through changing features of the environment. Having reached the fluid and uncertain context of our

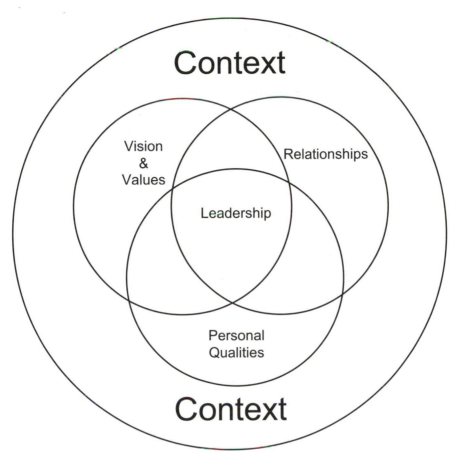

Figure 1

Table 2 – IMG Model

Vision and Values	Leaders embody the Vision and Values of the organisation	INSPIRE
Relationships	Leaders stimulate creativity by their relationships with others	MOTIVATE
Personal Attributes	Leaders creatively use personal and professional development as the key to growth – for the organization, for people, for themselves	GROW

modern world, we can use the features as core stabilising factors from which to develop responsive leadership. *Response-ability* to changing environments, cultures and climates is a marker of creativity in leadership.

CREATIVE LEADERSHIP THINKING SPACE

- Have you made the step change from management to leadership? Do you have the balance right?
- How well would you rate your *response-ability* to changing environments, cultures and climates?
- How can you match your leadership approach against the features of the IMG model?

Notes

1 Neil Dempster 2009:22
2 The work of Janet Taylor et al (2010) as reported by JohnJoe McFadden, Professor of Molecular Genetics at University of Surrey, *The Guardian*, Saturday 10 July 2010.
3 Pam Sammons et al. (1997)
4 Neil Dempster (2009:26)
5 Frank Coffield and Sheila Edwards (2009:371–390)
6 *Ibid* 2009:375
7 James C. Scott (1998)
8 Nani Beccalli (2004)
9 John West-Burnham (2009:65)
10 From personal communication with Gordon, Research and Consultancy Director.
11 Robert Sternberg 2005:347
12 Estyn 2011
13 Since the time I visited Ysgol Plasmawr, the Welsh inspectorate Estyn have introduced Wellbeing as a theme so all schools will have to take account of it.
14 Sami Abuhamdeh and Mihaly Csikszentmihalyi (2004:33)
15 Sir William Atkinson, Wales Education Lecture (2009:10)
16 Robert Sternberg (2005:359)

7

Inspire: Vision and Values

Write the vision, and make it plain upon tables, that he may run that readeth it.

HABAKKUK CH.2, V.2.

Chapter Outline

In one way, Vision and Values, as the *Inspire* element of the IMG framework, represent a first stage towards creative leadership. On the other hand, the whole model of Inspire – Motivate – Grow represents a seamless framework: there is an interdependency each on the other. Vision and Values will be empty gestures unless they are built into Relationships, and their credibility relies on the Personal Attributes of a leader to apply them as motivational force. But as the first step, this chapter will ask you to think about how you use Vision and Values in your leadership. Because Vision and Values are where leaders operate.

'Visionary' has been a word frequently applied to great leaders. It's an indicator of the crucial role of vision in leadership. Vision is something great leaders in history appear to have in common: the ability to conceive of futures beyond the imagination of us ordinary folk.

What marks leaders out as great has been their ability to articulate their personal vision to harness a movement towards its achievement. A vision phrased as 'I have a dream' by Martin Luther King indicates how interpretation of personal visions can become iconic statements forever linked with their initiator.

The ability to interpret a vision is imperative because leaders may need to exhort followers to expend exceptional effort in order to attain a better future. Prime Minister Winston Churchill famously offered the British people nothing but 'blood, toil, tears and sweat' during the Second World War. Visionary leaders are not only able to conceive of a future beyond the understanding of the rest of us; by their words and actions they are able to stimulate the energy to move towards its attainment.

Of course visions that generate a following are not always worthy or socially desirable. You could call a leader 'great' based on their ability to attract and energise large followings, but not necessarily 'good' if the cause is reprehensible. Historically, many a leaders' vision has led to undemocratic and de-humanising movements, even genocide.

That's why values are crucially linked to visions. A vision is an expression of values; it defines the values of a society or an organization, it provides a medium through which values can be channelled into identifiable achievements.

Having a vision is crucial to promoting and achieving change. The ability to define and promote a vision is a crucial difference between management and leadership. We can recognise visionary leaders when we see them, and there may be an assumption that such individuals are particularly and uniquely talented. But as we've been arguing that creativity is a universal human attribute there's no reason why we shouldn't be able to think and act creatively in respect of a vision for ourselves and our organization. By unpacking some of the mystique perhaps we can gain an understanding of the elements of creating a vision.

Clarity of vision is a professional act

Mal – Headteacher

Visions, goals and targets

The first thing to be clear about is the difference between a vision, a goal and a target. The roles are actually quite separate, yet without clear definition they become confused and the terms can even used interchangeably. **Table 3** provides a starting point towards a recognition of the differences.

An understanding of the difference between visions, goals and targets is important so that each can be accurately conveyed in language. Visions in particular, because of their perceived tenuous nature, can be notoriously difficult to put into words. Robert Dilts offers an illustration in the phrase 'Our mission is to be a professional organization that supports and provides for our members'. Robert suggests this is at best an 'identity' statement, because mission and vision are not self-serving. Rather mission and vision:

'...define the role of the individual or organization with respect to something beyond themselves. It is the service to something beyond the individual or organization that gives the "purpose" to "purposeful organisation"'.[1]

If a vision provides the *purpose*, a goal then provides the *motivation*. Albert Bandura shows there is now a large body of evidence to show that explicit, challenging goals can enhance and sustain motivation. Goals operate largely through influencing rather than regulating action directly.[2] And here again, how goals are framed will influence their potential to be achieved:

Table 3 Targets, Goals and Visions 1

Targets	Goals	Visions
Specific fixed points	Individually motivational	Broadly aspirational
Applied externally as markers of improvement	Stimulants for individual motivation	Shared creation that generates energy towards an exciting future
Explicit and static	Realistic and challenging	Holistic and vibrant
The domain of management	Shared responsibility	The domain of leadership
The effect is to channel work towards it, such as 'teaching to the test'	The effect is to mobilize the resources and effort needed to succeed	The effect is to unite the whole organization to a common theme

'If a goal is not REALISTIC, there is no hope, but if it is not CHALLENGING, there is no motivation. So there is an envelope here into which all goals should fit.'[3]

Targets then are the mechanism for regulating specific actions. Because they are specific, you might expect their expression to be quite straight-forward. Yet I have seen targets expressed so loosely in organizations that I have had to question how you would recognize if and when they were achieved. For instance 'Further develop the admissions procedure' is not a target. It's not time-related, and 'further develop' is meaningless as a guide to what has to be done. Neither is it a goal, if we take on board the recom-mendation that goals need to be Realistic and Challenging. At best, it is a mechanistic, procedural statement that is unlikely to engage the enthusiasm of those concerned with its implementation. Simon Caulkin is quite scathing in this respect, he writes that target-driven organisations are 'institutionally witless' because they face the wrong way; rather than facing customers and citizens, they serve ministers and target-setters.[4]

Yet in education, targets have become increasingly prevalent; for policy makers, target-setting and their achievement is seen as crucial to raising educational achievement. Target-setting has spawned a reliance on data to the degree that it can be said to have reached the level of an obsession. Data collection has its place: to know where you are going, you need an under-standing of where you are, so you know what you have to do to get there. But when the time and effort expended on data collection and meeting targets becomes the purpose of the work, there can be a danger of losing sight of the overall objective. Targets are just the stepping-stones to achieving a vision: they need to be in service to the vision, rather than becoming the tail that wags the dog of education.

Visions, goals and targets then all have their role to play, and the first learning point is that there are broad rules that apply to their expression in language. **Table 4** gives examples that might occur in the context of a further education college, and also reveals the second essential factor: the need for alignment between all three. The vision needs to be both potent and engaging in order to energize the whole organisation towards its achievement. It also serves as a reference point whereby those involved in setting goals and targets can 'chunk up' to check all aspects of the organization are aligned with the overall vision.

Table 4 – Targets, Goals, Visions 2

Definition		College Examples
The **purpose** of the organization in relation to a wider element	**VISION** ↑	Empowering young people to become confident, skilful and informed citizens
Broad outcome **indicators**	**GOALS** ↑ ↑ ↑	↑ 'Learner Voice' strategy established throughout the college ↑ Student achievement raised to improve progression in education or to employment ↑ Reduction in the 'churn'[1] of NEETs
Specific time-related **expectations**	**TARGETS** ↑ ↑ ↑ ↑ ↑	↑ Student course representatives recruited for all courses by third week of new academic year ↑ Improve results of annual student survey to ?% satisfaction ↑ Improve average student attainment in examinations to ?% by the end of the academic year ↑ Increase recruitment of NEETs into learning by ?% by [date] ↑ ?% of lecturers to have achieved Essential Skills Level 3 qualification by [date]

[1] Roll on – roll off engagement that keeps numbers static

The emotional element of visions

I've used the word 'aligned' up to now as a phrase often used in leadership when talking about engaging organisations in high level strategy. However, it doesn't really accommodate or represent the emotional element of work – the need for meaning and personal engagement that you read about in Chapter 2. Daniel Goleman feels *alignment* promotes a mechanical image of getting all the pencils pointing in the right direction; a dry language that only speaks to the rational brain.[5]

For Daniel Goleman, getting people to really embrace change requires *attunement,* a kind of resonance that moves people emotionally as well as intellectually. Attunement, rather than mere alignment, offers the motivating enthusiasm for an organisational vision:

'Emotionally intelligent leaders know that this attunement requires something more than simply making people aware of the strategy itself. It requires a direct connection with people's emotional centers…The invisible threads of a compelling vision weave a tapestry that binds people together more powerfully than any strategic plan. And people, not the business plan alone, determine the outcome.'[6]

Of course, if we're aiming for leadership to stimulate creativity in others, we have to acknowledge that people are different, and that therefore they will be motivated in different ways, and likely to respond emotionally to different stimuli. In particular, people who are already creative themselves are likely to be *self*-motivated, in which case the imposition of an external vision, if anything, might inhibit performance.[7]

And of course the vision is not solely for those within the school or college community; it needs to reach out and engage the wider community, parents and families, future students. This is where a danger arises that in order to be meaningful to a wide audience, the message becomes 'dumbed-down'. Howard Gardner has suggested we can see evidence of this in wider society; with information becoming a mass commodity, the media have been pushed to provide news that appeals to the broadest possible audience.[8]

Rather than 'dumbing-down', for both these reasons – to engage people who are already self-motivated **and** to be meaningful to a wide audience – a vision needs to be 'chunked up' to a level that makes it attractive to people by its universal appeal. It needs to be an articulation of some high level, 'taken-for-granted' element that engages people at an emotional level.

At the other end of the motivation spectrum of course are the people who lack self-motivation and rely upon external factors to motivate them to higher achievement. Howard Gardner points out that the path of least resistance – entropy or inertia – is constantly at work in history, as well as in the physical universe. When it comes to human affairs, overcoming entropy is not easy, and it takes not only faith in a vision of a better way to live but also a commitment to translating that vision into reality. A reliance upon the old signposts to the best direction may no longer be relevant, and may prove inadequate:

'If we wish to envision an alternative to inertia, we must consider which values could serve as a map to the future'.[9]

All religions have recognised that communities could be destroyed if everyone was motivated by sheer selfishness, so devised scenarios for what would happen to those who acted only in terms of self-interest – such as reincarnation into a lower form of life, or going to hell. All societies that survived have had to devise positive rules to direct the energy of people towards life-sustaining behaviours.[10]

John Adair suggests our capacity to value is innate, but our actual values are conditioned by our particular cultural situation in life.[11] Yet although values may feel like fundamentals that are deeply embedded in our cultures, they also evolve over time to fit with our knowledge of our world. With the benefit of hindsight, we can see that the culture of the 1980s that spawned a notion that 'greed is good' may have led to fiscal disasters on a global scale. In education, we no longer hold it acceptable that small children working 12-hour shifts in a factory or a mine is the 'right' thing to be doing. We are seeing values evolve in respect of the basis of the relationship between adults and children, and in respect of what education should be about. If the vision serves as a signpost to where we want to be going, values need to be an up-to-date guide book to a better future, rather than looking back over our shoulders

> *I really do believe in the transformational nature of education. It gives people a second chance. It's a wonderful thing to do to make people's lives different.*
>
> Dick – Principal of a Further Education College

Creating values

If the vision is what you want to accomplish, and goals and targets are what you have to do to achieve it, the glue that enables the whole thing to hang together is the answer to the question 'What is important?'

A quick trawl on the internet can reveal that all types of organization have given thought to the core values that underpin their operation, and set them out as steers to their work:

- Virgin Atlantic define their core values of **Safety, Security** and **Consistent Delivery** as the foundation of everything they do

- NASA base Mission Success on their core values of **Safety, Teamwork, Integrity** and **Excellence**

- RFU, the Governing Body of rugby union in the UK set up a task group consultation to define their core values: **Teamwork, Respect, Enjoyment, Discipline, Sportsmanship**

- The National Association of Social Workers envisage their profession rooted in core values of **Service, Social Justice, Dignity and Worth of the Person, Importance of Human Relationships, Integrity, Competence.**

So private and public sectors, sport and professions, all identify a value base for their operation. The above also shows that definitions can spill over from the more common three in number: an indicator that – as with visions, goals and targets – definition in language can be a challenging exercise.

For instance, consider this as a core value articulated by a UK education authority:

'The physical and social environment of the schools supports classroom teaching'.

Apart from being too wordy, this clearly doesn't engage at an emotional

---

Fairness – in all things, in decision-making, seeing that people have a fair deal. If they work hard they get recognized for it, children get a fair deal in school. Also ***respect*** *and* ***tolerance***.

Janet – Primary School Teacher

I have to have ***belief in the end goal*** *– I have to believe in it. It's the one underpinning value, it's fundamental.*

Sheelagh – Health Service Director

Values are critical. Personally, I'm in favour of the ***moral purpose for education***.

David – Director of an Institute for Applied Education Research

The most important values that influence my headship? Ones ***in tune with professionality***.

Richard – Primary Headteacher

Integrity, Trust, Respect for individuals. *And* ***Passion*** *for making things better for students – which means you may ruffle feathers*

Gloria – HM Inspector

level; it's really a goal rather than a value. So compare the above with the core values of a further education college:

Inspirational – Inclusive – Influential.

Values may need to be catchy and memorable in order to be attractive to a wide range of stakeholders. But at the same time they need to represent some fundamental conviction that we hold to be true. They are not a description of our behaviour, rather they act as a guide to our behaviour and decision-making, our beliefs about what is possible, attainable and desirable.[12]

As the examples above show, the leaders interviewed for this book had no problem answering my question 'What values underpin your leadership?', as they had clearly defined their personal values. It also became evident that their personal values were 'acted out' in their professional behaviours, even if it meant they had to take challenging decisions.

Personal values may not be an issue that we ponder over consciously on a daily basis, but the power of their conviction should not be underestimated. I have known people who have made dramatic changes of course in their careers because the values of the organization or management they were working for were in conflict with their personal value base. John West-Burnham argues that it's not that every leader should be a paragon, but rather that their actions should be seen to be ethically based, value driven and morally consistent.[13] And it's the 'seen to be' part that is crucial: as you will see below, it is not just what the values are, but how you *interpret* them.

Leaders as values role models

Vision and values are where leaders operate. Leaders define what is possible. They use a vision to inspire and values to energise by giving people something worthy to spend their time working towards.

Leaders do not just articulate a vision and values. They act as role models so people can experience the vision and values represented in action. If anything, it could be argued that this is more important in education than other professions. It is the reason why all teachers are leaders, because in all their behaviours they are modelling personal, professional and organizational values.

At a personal level, values may not be things we have consciously thought about very often. But they are an integral part of us, part of our understanding of the world. They have been distilled from our early life experiences and our culture. We will be influenced by people we interact with, by what we have read and seen on television, by the Code of Practice of our profession. Our values can be recognised in our behaviour, in the language we use and in the way we deal with people. And they may surface when we meet a situation that we instinctively feel is 'not right', when we might have to grapple with something that challenges our 'conscience'.

Values are strongly influencing drivers of action. The one thing the leaders interviewed for this book had in common was that they had thought about the values that guided their leadership to the extent that they were able to follow them through in their leadership behaviours. Sheelagh, for instance, had been prompted to move back to the public sector because working for a publisher didn't fit with her personal value of needing the end goal of her work to fit with what she valued as worthwhile. She could believe in a value of improving patient care, but as she said 'I couldn't get excited about selling newspapers'.

Daniel Goleman also makes the point that, while values may change over time, what is more enduring is an underlying personal philosophy that dictates how we *interpret* our values. He gives examples of one individual who lists 'family' as a dominant value, yet who spends five days a week away from his wife and family travelling for his job. His 'acting out' of this value is by providing enough money for his family. In contrast, and manager who also declares 'family' as a value has turned down promotions in order to have dinner each night with his wife and children.[14]

The whole debate about what education is for, is an interpretation of values. I have seen college principals and school heads who appear to espouse similar values in relation education, but whose leadership could not be more different. A college principal who claims 'learners first' demonstrates this in a pragmatic style based on goal-setting and the efficiency of the college, with an intolerance of consensual leadership. Conversely, a primary school head who espouses 'learners first' offers no coherent discipline policy, relying upon one-to-one informal chats with miscreants.

In both these cases there has been an impact, both on the culture of the organization, and upon staff members. There have been losses to both organizations from professional and effective individuals feeling moved to resign due to a mismatch between the resultant culture and their own personal values.

Clearly then it is not enough to maintain a strong personal value base in leadership. What marks an individual out as a leader is that they create 'followship'. Unless there is a consensus on the interpretation of a values base for an organization it will cause a dissonance in the culture, and be likely to impact upon good working relationship for individuals.

The leader's role in both defining and 'acting out' the values of an organization is therefore crucial to overall success. As social analyst Richard Sennett has written, values are not abstract imperatives: they are evident in the actions of everyday life, and they can be recognized in language and behaviour.[15]

The process towards a value-based operation needs thought and consultation; a process that can be described in straightforward steps: from the personal, through the organisational, to the action.

Step One – The Personal

Values do not just change in cultures, they change for individuals as well. Frequently there are external pressures that dictate to us what we *ought* to be and do, influences that deflect us from the deeper, more challenging drive to realise our 'ideal' selves.[16] People can operate under a set of values that on a conscious level they *think* they espouse, only to find when a situation arises that challenges their 'acquired' values, it forces them to rethink the basis of their life and work.

Sheelagh is not alone in changing her career path for a more personally satisfying direction. James in Chapter 2 had trained to be a barrister to please his father, but gained no professional satisfaction from a legal career. He gave up everything and lived on credit for two years in order to achieve his ambition to be a renowned chef. My colleague Nigel had trained as an accountant because at school he was 'good at maths' and his teachers had influenced his decision. In the course of his career he was drawn to move from private practice into teaching because he recognised that working with people was more meaningful for him than working with figures.

Gaining clarity about personal values may develop over years before decisive change comes about. But for leaders, that clarity needs to be gained purposefully if they are to develop the values of their organization in a way that is professionally meaningful. *Step One* therefore involves taking some time and space to reflect on the values that guide your life and work, and Exercise 1 suggests a structured process to enable you to do this.

Practice Point 1 – Eliciting personal values

Think about the question 'What's important to me about leadership in education?

Write down single words or phrases that are the important things to you about leadership in education.
    Read out the words to yourself.

When you've written all you can think of, double-check by asking yourself 'What *else* is important to me about leadership in education?'

And is there *anything else* that is important to you about leadership in education?

Read over the list again and think about, if you were only allowed to have *one* of the items, which would you choose? Write it down.

Then if you were allowed to have *just one more* of the items, which would you choose? Write it down.

And if you were allowed to have *another* of the items, which would it be? Continue your second list.

And what would be the *next* item you would choose that's important to you about leadership in education?

Work your way through your first list until you make the final choice to add to your second list.

Is there a difference in the order of items on your first and second lists?

If there is a difference in the order, has this made you think any differently about what's important to you about leadership in education?

What would you now say are your three key personal values in relation to leadership in education?

Step Two – The Organisational

When Malcolm became a college principal for the first time he made a point of meeting up with all the teams and asking them the same questions: What is the college good at? What needs to improve? What would you not want to lose?

At one level these questions will generate practical answers on specific functional areas of a school or college's work. But they are also values questions. They enable a new leader to assess what is important to people, to gain insight into the culture and to open up reflection and discussion on organizational values.

It's not only leaders new to headships that need to establish the values of their organization. Two years into his headship of a secondary school Phil recognized a need to review the focus of the whole school. It had been an under-achieving school when he'd been appointed: he'd tackled the outstanding issues, in the process some staff had left and other new people had been appointed. With results starting to improve, he felt he was beginning to turn the school around. But he had a sense that in concentrating on the urgent he had neglected the important: he needed to align the culture under a vision and values to achieve a step-change in improvement.

Given the pressures upon schools and colleges, it may appear a luxury to take time away from urgent tasks at hand. But time spent creating a vision and value base is an investment that pays future dividends. Phil initiated a consultation that involved all members of the school. Posing the question 'What core values do we want to take our school forward to the future?' staff were invited to contribute to the heads blog, leaders were asked to garner views at team meetings, and management meetings had a discussion of values as an item on the agenda. Members of the School Council were tasked with leading the debate amongst the students to encourage them to submit views via the school website. Finally a staff training day was held to draw all views together, and to tease out how the core values of Respect – Aspire – Achieve could be actioned throughout the school.

Time taken to create a following behind a vision and values is only an investment if it is followed through to the next stage. Schools and colleges may proclaim their vision and values on their website, signage and letter-headings, but it is for a leader to ensure that values are demonstrated in action. And as you will see in the next section, their interpretation forms a reference point for the quality of the organisation.

Practice Point 2 – Eliciting other people's values

Practice Point 1 is an illustration that eliciting core values is not always as straightforward as asking a direct question. Our core values may direct our behaviour and our choices in life, but they can be difficult to articulate because we don't often think about them until we come up against a situation that presents a challenge. But a leader will need to generate an open discussion in order to define the values of their organisation. For this, skilful questioning will involve using open questions, avoiding influencing the responses by the way the questions are constructed or how they are asked.

Values that people hold to be important can be revealed in the way people talk about their life and work. One way to encourage open discussion is by use of the 'Miracle Question'.[17] You could use this with any individual or group; my example below is an illustration of how I used it for interviewing groups of 15-year-old students on what they thought about their school.

'Imagine' I said to the young people, 'that when you go to bed tonight, while you are asleep a miracle occurs. When you wake up tomorrow morning you don't know a miracle has happened because it happened while you were sleeping. But the miracle has been that everything about school has been changed for the better. What would you notice that would tell you that the miracle had occurred? What would be different? And what else...?'

As long as you keep listening, encouraging responses with a regular input of 'And what else...' you'll find that this question gives people free rein to express what is important to them. The young people in this case had no problem coming up with practical suggestions on what would improve their school life: fairer organization at lunch time so they weren't always last in the queue, have lockers so they didn't have to carry heavy bags round with them all day, better range of food on offer in the canteen. Get rid of the pond in the garden because it might pose a danger for younger pupils. Teachers should be 'safe', they should listen more; even one suggestion that the teacher should be in the middle of the room, rather than always at the front.

Consider: Looking at how these young people have described their 'ideal' school, what would you say were the values that underpin their ideas. What values you can list as important to these young people?

Stage Three – The Action

Michael Mumford has pointed out that it's questionable whether visionary leadership has much relevance to creative leadership. As previously mentioned, people who are already creative are likely to be self-motivated, in which case the imposition of an external vision could, if anything, inhibit performance.[18] So if one of the overall aims for creative leadership in education is to develop creative people, this is an important point to be borne in mind.

Rather, the suggestion is that a leader's vision can exert lasting indirect effect by shaping decisions around procedures and goals. Leaders can build a creative culture and climate by framing decisions, not just in objective terms, but in terms of the impact of these decisions upon the values espoused by the organization:

'...over time, the framing of decisions in terms of the climatic variables shaping creativity and innovation may represent one of the more powerful effects of leadership on the innovative capacity of the organization.'[19]

Translating this in terms of decision-making within a school or college was exactly what Rob did during his tenure as an Acting Principal. The senior management team used the college's mission of 'Learners First' as a reference point for decision-making. Where decisions were problematic, the final deciding factor was always, 'what's best for the learner?' Further, when difficult decisions were passed to others for action, this rationale was shared, disseminating the mission throughout the college.

Clarity about values can also stimulate creative responses when frustration or disappointments occur. Teachers will recognize that cohorts of students vary: one year a class will progress easily in their learning, there will be a comfortable match between what the teacher is providing and the learning attainment of the students; the following year a class may struggle, unable to match the expectations of the teacher. One response could be 'stick to the lesson plan, it's worked before, this must just be a class who don't pick things up quickly'. But where a value base of putting learners first is instilled into practice, the response is more likely to be 'what do I need to do differently to help these young people to learn'. In this way, values are not only 'acted out', they provide an impetus for creativity.

It is this 'acting out' feature of values in action that is a crucial medium for the dissemination of values. A leader's behaviour will be open to scrutiny at all times. We've all had the experience of hearing someone say something, but intuitively feeling they didn't really mean it. Subtle 'leakage' via body language channels signal whether what someone is saying is what they really think and believe in. Values may be publicly proclaimed in a school's materials, but if the leader doesn't demonstrate them in their language and behaviour, they will be no more than empty words. Values are the glue that holds everything together, the energy that drives motivation to achieve a vision, and the foundation of the behaviours featured in the next two chapters.

Practice Point 3 – Acting on values

What are the practical ways your organisation uses core values as a reference point for its work?

How are the core values disseminated throughout the organization to provide a common reference point?

What could be done to encourage people to 'act on values'?

Have you had the experience of changing a decision after relating the issue to core values?

Describe ways the in which your behaviour is role-modelling values for colleagues and young people .

Inspire: Vision and values for creative leadership

During my interview with him, David joked that one time if a principal said he had a vision he'd be locked up – now he's expected to have a vision. The vision of a leader can indeed have powerful effects, and an example from the corporate world illustrates the extent of the effect achievable from leading by vision and values.

Steve Jobs was described as a 'creative visionary' who was able to create a vision for Apple that cascaded throughout the organization without losing intensity. Jobs also demonstrated how persistent adherence to values – in his case an obsessive culture of perfection – made Apple a world-leader. Further than that, discussions on his legacy have credited him with, not only changing the business world, but changing the way we all view technology, the way we communicate, the way we think about design and invention, and much more.[20]

If we then look at education, vision and values feature prominently in research into how innovative, self-improving colleges achieve their award-winning status. Interviews with 17 leaders in the college sector by the Association of Colleges revealed that they gave powerful messages about their colleges' values, leading by example through direct involvement and support for innovation. All placed importance upon helping staff to understand 'this is how we do things', and to work out what that meant for their practice. Clarity about their colleges' values and mission was translated into distinct expectations of staff, students, and themselves. College principals also recognised they needed leaders at every level. Award-winning curriculum leaders were the yeast in successful colleges – helping the whole organization to rise. They have the vision of what can be achieved, and the credibility and skills to take their team with them.[21]

The influence of vision and values then is not to be under-estimated. They provide the *Inspire* element of the creative leadership framework, not only for leadership of an organisation, but with the potential to impact upon a much wider sphere. For educators, there is the potential to spread the Inspire influence to young people, families, local communities, the political sphere. An influence, indeed, not to be underestimated.

> *You have to create an environment that is focused on student achievement.*
>
> David – Director of Institute of Applied Education Research

Leadership is also 'walking the talk'.

Gordon – Research and Consultancy Director

I believe in sharing a collective vision that we can all sign up to. People will have different values – some are not negotiable, others can be shaped by consultation.

Paul – Health Service Executive

Showing respect for people. For people to trust me.

Maria – Faculty Head

Respect – I wouldn't dream of raising my voice even with people who have made real real mistakes. Enjoying the working day – which will influence the students. Reflecting before making a decision; making decisions with the best of intentions. Always bringing decisions back to the student – what will be the impact and will it be for their benefit.

Kay – Faculty Director

Professionalism is about having a clear vision that is communicated to staff and engages them. You have to 'walk the talk'.

Dick – College Principal

As long as I'm convinced staff have been trying to do something and make a mistake, that's OK. Staff that let kids down make me very angry and disappointed. Badly prepared lessons for example. Responding to kids is one of the kindest things we do. Once kids think you value them and their work you've got them.

Mal – Headteacher

CREATIVE LEADERSHIP THINKING SPACE

- Is *everyone* in the organisation clear about the overall vision? Do they understand their role in fulfilling the vision?

- Are the values used as a benchmark in decision-making?

- Are your personal values in tune with the values of the organisation?

- Do you talk about values so that their interpretation is consistent?

- Do you 'walk the talk'?

- How do you disseminate the vision and values of your organisation within your local community? Is the message clear and unambiguous, and supported by the actions of everyone in the organization?

Notes

1 Robert Dilts 1996:79
2 Albert Bandura 1995:7
3 John Whitmore 2002:61–62
4 Simon Caulkin 2009
5 Daniel Goleman 2002:208
6 *Ibid.* 2002:208-9
7 Michael Mumford et al. 2002:738
8 Howard Gardner et al. 2001:230
9 *Ibid.* p. 237
10 Mihaly Csikszentmihalyi 1997:140
11 John Adair 2009:69
12 Full a full exposition, see Mark Halstead and Monica Taylor, 1996 *Values in Education and Education in Values*
13 John West-Burnham 2009:65
14 Daniel Goleman 2002:122
15 Richard Sennett 2010:26
16 Daniel Goleman 2002:115–19
17 The 'Miracle Question' was created by Steve de Shazer, originator of Solution-Focused Brief Therapy, adapted from a strategy used by Milton Erickson.
18 Michael Mumford et al. 2002:738
19 *Ibid.* 2002:733
20 Julian Baggini 2011
21 http://www.aoc.co.uk/en/aoc_beacon_gold_and_other_awards/aoc_beacon_gold_awards/celebrating-colleges/winning-capabilities/visionary_leadership.cfm accessed 5 September 2011

8

Motivate: Relationships

Having stressed the importance of Vision and Values for creative leadership, this chapter now explores how the behaviour of a leader influences and motivates. Leaders act as role models so people can experience the Vision and Values represented in action. It is the interpersonal skills of the leader that invest the Vision and Values with a compelling force that aligns the energy of the organization towards their fulfilment. Building relationships may involve practice, but the most important thing is that they don't depend upon being a certain type of person: rather they depend upon skills that can be learned. The importance of the skills is that leadership may need a *context* to be evident, but it also needs *relationships* to be apparent. For Joseph O'Connor leadership does not exist as an independent quality, it only exists between people: it describes a relationship.[1] Relationships within education are changing: a creative leader needs to be able to adapt and develop their relationship skills if they are to motivate others to fulfil their own creative capacity.

When my first son started primary school, if you wanted to see the headmaster you always knew where to find him. He would be in his office, door closed, seated behind his desk. A very tidy desk as I recall, bare of piles of papers, usually just one working paper in front of him.

When my youngest son started at the same school ten years later there was a different head – by now a headteacher rather than a master. And not so easy to find him if you wanted a word. He would either be in a classroom talking to a teacher, or taking football practice, or meeting with Parent Teacher Association members to talk about their next fund-raising project.

My sons are adults now and I haven't met the current head of the school. But I've heard about her. She's well-known in the local community because of the activities she engages in. She joined the local Rotary Club for instance and secured a donation of reading books for the school.

I suppose this personal history is indicative of the changes in school leadership over the years: from a head being a distant figure of authority, working in isolation; to becoming more engaged in the work of teachers and drawing parents into involvement with the school; to extending the leadership role outside the school to the local context and wider. It's one illustration of how the main change in leadership has been to relationships.

The other aspect of the changing relationships of course is that leadership is no longer seen to be vested in a single individual. A response to complexity, both of our modern world and of educational organizations, has been a movement to a notion of 'distributed' leadership: an acknowledgement that leadership needn't be restricted to one type of person in a particular management role, exhibiting a particular set of skills and attributes. This book has been written for all teachers because all teachers are leaders: they may not hold a 'management' post but in their relationships with young people, parents, colleagues, they will be sharing leadership. Neil Dempster writes of this change from a concentration on leadership as individual action to leadership as collective activity, and believes it is a change in the right direction.[2]

It's also important to acknowledge the relationships aspect of leadership because experience and research suggests that, where problems in organizations occur, it is frequently due to a failure in relationships. The people and contexts may be different, but the principles appear to be the same: when difficulties occur, there has often been a breakdown in relationships, a lack of clarity about roles and relationships, or an inability to handle conflicts of interest.[3]

Leadership today then, is a social activity. And as you saw in Chapter Five, creativity also is described as both a mental and social process. So leadership and creativity come together in the facilitation of positive and productive relationships, providing the *Motivation* aspect of the IMG model. *Inspire* generates the Vision, *Motivation* then encourages people to act on the Vision: teachers motivating students and parents, Heads and Principals establishing relationships within which the intrinsic motivation of creative staff is nurtured and encouraged.

The impact of relationships

Changes in relationships generally in the western world have brought about significant changes to relationships in education. Julian Elliott and his colleagues have pointed out that teachers can no longer depend upon their traditional authority, rather the emphasis has shifted to the development and exercise of professional skills. For student teachers, without the authoritative status of previous years to underpin their practice, it is hardly surprising that behaviour management has become an area where it's recognised that they have much to learn. In addition, student teachers' individual development will be closely linked to the development of professional relationships in their school, and they will rarely have had any significant training in working with parents.[4]

It's in these areas – developing professional relationships and working with parents – that student teachers rely upon the knowledge of more experienced teachers acting as school-based mentors. The difficulty is that this is tacit knowledge; experienced teachers may have learned how to develop good relationships, but they are unlikely to be able to describe exactly what they do. As mentioned in Chapter 2, it's this sort of complex professional behaviour that's difficult to break down into individual competences, or even to describe. Skilled interpersonal performance involves not only the selection of an appropriate strategy in a given situation, but the capacity to carry it out effectively. And this is only one aspect of skilled performance in relationships: an experienced teacher can often *prevent* problems from occurring in the first place by their skilful use of their voice and non-verbal behaviour, and their ability to handle multiple events concurrently.[5]

I'm reminded here of when Rachael was in her first year of teaching at primary school. She loved interacting with the children, but at first felt quite nervous and unsure about how to deal with parents. With experience she discovered that most parents were friendly and supportive, and interested in their child's well-being. But there's always the exception, and for Rachael it was a mother who always seemed to be looking for an argument, who'd already had run-ins with the head and her social worker. She regularly turned up at the classroom door with some complaint or other, and Rachael confessed that on one occasion she'd hid in the store cupboard rather than face her.

If student teachers have little initial guidance or preparation in dealing with difficult relationships, plainly this is an area that depends upon experience to develop expertise. But there are other factors that impact upon the possibility of developing skilled performance. Even the experienced teachers in Julian Elliot's study admitted that, although they could distinguish between sound or poor strategies, even they sometimes responded inappropriately in a difficult situation due to emotion, stress or frustration.[6]

So if even experienced teachers do not always opt for an appropriate response, what will set a creative leader apart in the area of relationships? Despite the difficulty of *describing* complex professional behaviours, experience tells me it is possible to *model* the fine detail of interpersonal behaviours, and you will find examples in what follows.

However, acquiring new behavioural strategies is not the complete answer. Daniel Goleman writes that the triad of emotional intelligence attributes – self-awareness, self-management and empathy – come together in relationship management. Because being able to manage relationships skilfully boils down to handling the emotions of others, it follows that leaders have to be aware of their own emotions and feel empathy for the people they lead.[7]

Real empathy is not an attitude that can be put on externally like a coat. It's something that emerges from a genuine deeply held concern. Without that, attempts to demonstrate empathy will be recognised for what they are – just a façade. Daniel Goleman writes that empathy represents a necessary ingredient of emotionally intelligent leadership, and:

'…another lies in leaders' ability to express their message in a way that moves others. Resonance flows from a leader who expresses feelings with conviction because those emotions are clearly authentic, rooted in deeply held values.'[8]

Practice Point 4

One way to resolve how to build a relationship with 'difficult' people is to separate the behaviour from the person. Whether they are being negative, obstructive, demanding or displaying any sort of behaviour that makes it difficult for you to build a productive relationship, that is just their *behaviour*, and their behaviour is not who they are. Building a relationship within which their behaviour can be changed will only be achieved by dealing with them as a *person* with empathy and respect.

So, think about someone you find challenging to work with. Perhaps there is someone you are hesitating to raise issues with because you fear their reaction.

Now think about their *behaviour*: what is it about the way they talk and act that makes it difficult to get along with them?

Next think about them as a *person:* what might it be about this person that makes them respond in the way they do? Might it be that they are afraid of something, might they be unsure of themselves, might it be the only way they know how to behave?

Finally, think about how you can respond to this *person* with empathy and respect. What do you need to do to show this person your positive regard for them as a person?

Linking values to interpersonal behaviour

You will have gained a sense of the power of values-driven behaviour from Chapter Seven. Vision and Values are where leaders operate; leaders act as role models so people can experience the vision and values represented in action. Values are also strongly influencing drivers of action.

There's an illustration of values in action in the continuing account of how Rachael overcame her fear and was able to deal with a really problematic issue concerning the 'difficult' parent. The stimulus came about because of Rachael's concern for the welfare of the child concerned. The little girl was overweight, was the only child in the class without a school uniform, and she would frequently turn up for school unwashed. Isolated by her classmates, she would stand alone in the yard, and more recently when sat at her desk, she had laid her head on her arms and burst into tears.

Rachael's concern for the child's well-being was genuine. But the headteacher and social worker – both experienced professionals – had already tried to intercede with the mother to improve conditions for the child, without success. So how could Rachael, in her first year of teaching, hope to make a difference?

But the depth of her concern overrode other considerations. With parent's evening approaching, Rachael sought advice on an appropriate strategy to raise her concerns with the parent. The interesting thing is that she was surprisingly successful. The mother even commented that she'd enjoyed talking to Rachael – better than talking to 'that headteacher' – and she felt they understood each other. More importantly, there was a practical result to the relationship: the child arrived at school the next day in a clean uniform, hair washed and generally spruced up.[9]

The 'difference that made the difference' was that Rachael was able to demonstrate empathy with the parent. The depth of her concern for the child gave her the motivation to overcome her fear and enough self-confidence to tackle a difficult topic of conversation. Her concern for the child was a deeply-held value, and because of this she came across as genuine and authentic, and matched at some level the concern of the parent. She was able to establish empathy with the parent based on a shared concern for the well being of the child, and the strength of her concern enabled her to express this in a way that moved the parent to action.

Just one interview, but it was the source of considerable personal and professional development for a newly qualified teacher. Indeed, Daniel Goleman's view is that handling relationships is not as simple as it sounds. Socially-skilled leaders need to have resonance with a wide circle of people; to have the knack of finding common ground and building rapport. It's not just a matter of friendliness, rather 'friendliness with a purpose';[10] the purpose being to fulfil the leadership role.

The skills of relationship management – Rapport

We can talk easily about the need to build rapport, but in reality it's often treated as something that either just exists, or doesn't exist between people. But because its influence shouldn't be underestimated, rapport warrants special attention. It is, after all, the building block of good relationships: 'a prerequisite to good communication, influence and change'.[11]

We can recognise that with some people, rapport seems to 'just happen' without effort on our part. Sometimes we may meet people for the first time, but it feels like we've known them for years. At a very basic level, we get along with people who we recognize are like ourselves at some level. With others, the relationship may not feel quite as comfortable, we may feel it takes some effort just to get along with them. And there will be yet other people who we think are just difficult, whatever we do or say, we just don't seem to be able to get on to their wavelength.

We use 'rapport' as a noun, however we need to recognise it as a *process*. It's on-going, dynamic and it can change. We may feel we are getting along with someone, when apparently for no reason at all, the relationship seems to sour. Plainly the best strategy would be to re-establish rapport, and make efforts to maintain it. But frequently – either through lack of will or lack of experience and skills – this doesn't happen. Sadly, I have seen breakdowns in relationships escalate to become serious situations; situations which could have been avoided with attention given to creating rapport in the first instance.

For me, writing about rapport brings to mind the words of Tim Brighouse describing the 'something more' that defined creative teachers. Reflecting upon the early years of his career, he recalled primary school teacher Mrs Lewis who, he said, would probably have identified 'personalisation' with number plates or cufflinks. Yet in the sense intended by current policy makers, she certainly practised 'personalisation'. She was at pains to deploy all the behaviours which made her practice 'personal' rather than 'impersonal'. In this respect, he felt, it was easier for Mrs Lewis than for her secondary school colleagues: often having to teach 200–300 different young people every week. Yet they put in the preparation to enable them to put names to faces so they could speak to young people by name in corridors at breaks as well as in lessons. Even so, every teacher will have encountered students with whom – despite their best efforts – rapport seems difficult to establish. Tim Brighouse described how creative teachers find ways to overcome this:

'When these teachers encounter a pupils with whom they cannot connect – whose mind and heart they do not meet – they go out of their way at the weekend to find an artefact or an article that is related to the youngster's private interest and on the Monday, they stop them in the corridor and say "Sean, I saw this and thought of you" '.[12]

Building rapport by remembering names

Early in my career I worked for a national charity concerned with the welfare of children and young people, based at their regional office in my home town. My first week with the organization coincided with a visit from the London-based national director. Along with other staff, I was invited to meet him informally over coffee. As a newcomer I felt quite nervous – he was after all the top man in the organisation – but he had a relaxed manner that put me at my ease, and I chatted with him for about five minutes.

I had a week's induction into the work of the region, then some three months later I was allocated a place on a national training course, which meant a week's stay in the London. There were six of us on the course, drawn from various parts of the UK. Despite our various backgrounds, we quickly bonded in the shared experience of being new to the organization, and extended our relationship into socialising in the evenings.

About the middle of the week, we were transferring from our training room to another part of the building, making our way along a corridor. It was long and quite narrow so we were walking single file, with me in the lead. Ahead of us, I spotted the national director, walking towards us. I was quickly running through in my head what might be an appropriate form of greeting: probably not 'Hi', would 'Good morning' be better, and should I use his name? But as we got close, he spoke first, 'Good morning Jacquie'.

Considering I'd met him only once, for about five minutes, and this was three months later, I thought it was fairly impressive he appeared to remember my name. I suppose you could suggest that perhaps he'd had a list of our names provided by his PA. But he still had to remember which one I was to use my name.

Whatever, it impressed me, just remembering my name was enough to make me warm to him. It even made an impression on my fellow trainees, who followed me whispering down the corridor, 'How did he know your name? How did he do that?'

Only a small incident, but it's stuck with me over many years as an illustration of how a small thing can have a big effect.

Practice Point 5: You can develop your ability to remember people's names by associating them mentally with something that will trigger the memory. When I met George, the name suggested 'King' to me, so I pictured him wearing golden crown. The first time I met Sue, she was telling the group how she had problems with delivery of a new sofa, so I filed away an image of her sat on a blue sofa.

Having improved your memory, take the opportunity to use people's names, particularly if you've only met them once before. And if you have to raise a difficult issue with someone, using their name *first* can make the message more acceptable, e.g. 'Paul, I'd like to talk about how we can improve Year 6's reading assessments'.

Where rapport happens effortlessly and unconsciously it's because we respond to people who are similar to ourselves. We can feel an affinity when we recognize people think like us, that they like the things we like, that they hold similar values to our own. Where that connection doesn't happen, teachers such as in Tim Brighouse's example, recognize the fundamental importance of *creating* rapport as the first step in building relationships.

For a leader, relationships will need to be built with a range of people, people who won't necessarily all be those who they might instantly warm to as individuals. And since we are generally consciously unaware of the factors that contribute to a connection between people, it can mean 'making the unconscious conscious' by raising awareness of what is happening in the process of rapport.

Being aware is the first step; as you will see in the examples below, the next step is actively 'matching' to create a connection.

Matching values

Chapter Seven featured the role of a leader in defining and role-modelling the values of their organization. A key factor was the role of the leader in interpreting the values of the organisation: ensuring that the values of the organisation and those of followers were aligned and in tune. Leadership is about inspiring people through a shared set of values.[13] It's about stimulating a sense of collective mission to carry the work of the organization forward. And maintaining rapport is a way to synchronise the different values and meanings of human beings.[14]

You have also seen that matching values creates an emotional connection. We can talk of leaders in terms of strategy, vision, or powerful ideas, but Daniel Goleman asserts the reality is much more primal: great leadership works through the emotions.[15]

On a person-to-person level, in the example of Rachael above, she was able to match values to create a positive personal relationship. Matching the parents' concern for her child established a rapport that meant Rachael could get a difficult message across to the parent.

When people's behaviour is problematic it may take a little effort to peel back the layers of surface behaviour and discover a common value. If the values of another person are not overtly evident, it may need some questioning, e.g. 'John, what's the most important thing for you in this?'

Focusing on values avoids falling into the trap of having a disagreement over details escalating into an argument. Discussions can soon get stuck when people start using phrases like 'I hear what you're saying, but...' You may think that saying this is acknowledging the other person's position. However, what that 'but' is doing is changing the meaning to 'I hear what you're saying *and* I don't agree with you'. Using 'but' is a barrier to progress; discussions can degenerate to heated exchanges from the frustration of being unable to get past the to'ing and fro'ing of 'yes...butting'.

Many times, disagreements may only be over the detail of an issue. So matching values helps people to recognize where the areas of agreement lie, rather than focusing on the areas in dispute. As a creative leader, you can demonstrate your role in defining values by the way you use language: 'It seems to me we both want the same from this, we just have different views on how to get there. How can we pool our ideas so we achieve our outcome'?

Matching words

To be able to match people in their experience, you need to notice more about them. As you become more aware of the people you interact with, you will begin to consciously note the individual differences in how people talk and act. You will notice that some people use particular words and phrases so regularly you can almost predict what they will say – as with Michael and Neil in Chapter 5.

The words people use also give a clue to *how* people are thinking as well as what they are thinking about. Consider phrases such as 'I see what you mean', 'That's not clear to me', 'I need to see it in black and white', 'I can see the point of this', 'Can you show me what you mean?', 'We need to focus on...' A repeated use of words relating to 'seeing' can suggest a person who favours visualisation as a thinking process – who needs to 'get the picture' to be able to understand.

On the other hand you may notice phrases such as 'Something tells me it won't work', 'I like the sound of that', 'That's music to my ears', 'I need to talk about this'. These might all be indicators of a person who is tuned in to the sounds of speech and gets their understanding from talking things through.

Then of course, there are phrases like 'I can't grasp the issue here', 'I like concrete ideas I can get to grips with', 'I can't put a handle on this', 'I've got a feeling...' All suggest a person processing their thinking by means of feelings and physical sensations, someone who would need to 'make sense' of an idea to understand it.

We all use these modes in our thinking. Our experience of the world outside us comes via our senses – what we see, hear, feel, taste and smell – then we *re-present* the way we experience that reality mentally using the same processes. Thus, thoughts are not just comprised of words, they are *activities*.[16]

We all use these activities of thinking, and for some of us there may be a favoured mode that, from an early age, we've come to rely upon. Once you're alert to these differences and able to detect patterns in language it opens up another means of creating rapport.

Matching other people's language needs to be done subtly and with care. It would be counterproductive to come across as mimicking or aping the way another person speaks. The purpose after all is to create an affinity: to connect to people by speaking the same language. And sometimes this needs no more than matching phrases as in 'I see...', 'That sounds good...', 'That feels right...'.

Matching voice

A clinic nurse in a training session once told me what she had noticed about a consultant she worked for. The female consultant spent a day in clinic seeing patients with half-hourly appointments. As individuals, the patients would all be very different: male or female, different in age and social background. What the nurse noticed was that for each one, the consultant adjusted her voice to match that of the particular patient.

One patient was an elderly lady; the doctor's tone was gentle and quite quiet. Another was a businessman; her tone became brisk and more staccato. With an animated female patient, the tempo speeded up, then slowed when she spoke with a young male showing signs of nervousness.

It's not certain whether the doctor was consciously matching the voices of her patients, or whether it was her natural style in creating rapport. What *is* certain, is that none of the patients felt anything unnatural was happening. Only the nurse, who was there throughout the day, detected the difference and noted it as a potential strategy for creating rapport with different people.

Matching body language

I was once training a group of teachers in managing relationships and I used my usual strategy of demonstrating 'how not to' as a way of opening up discussion on the 'how to'. Using an obliging volunteer from the group I ran through an interview acting out all the worse features of interpersonal behaviour – interrupting, looking at my watch, harsh voice tone, etc., etc. The group had no problem identifying the 'bad' features. One teacher recognised so much she was prompted to ask how I knew her Principal!

Then I re-ran the same scenario to demonstrate a more productive interview. As part of it, I deliberately sat in a way that matched the way my companion was seated: leaning slightly toward her, legs crossed at the same angle, small movements of hand to match her gestures.

Again, no problem for the group to spot the differences. Then one teacher pondered, did I know that I had my legs crossed the same way as my companion, and would that have made a difference? When I explained that matching the position of my partners' legs was part of the demonstration, she affected surprise: 'You mean you did that *deliberately*?'

It can feel strange to think of purposely matching another persons' physical stance and movements: but matching another persons' body language can be one of the easier ways to create rapport. The way we use our body becomes so familiar to us that it can feel uncomfortable to step outside and do something different. A 'closed' body position for instance (legs crossed and arms folded) may feel a comfortable way to sit for one person, but to another person it may look and feel like a lack of receptiveness. In this respect, self awareness needs to extend to our whole demeanour: First thinking about the messages our own body is sending out, then adjusting your positioning or gestures in some way to match the other person.

As with language, matching body position and gestures needs to be subtle to be effective. And probably the most subtle mode of matching in this respect lies in matching breathing. People who enjoy singing may tell you that there's more to membership of a choir than just a group of people singing the same music. There's something about singing together in harmony that breeds a fellowship above and beyond the physical membership. And the fact that our word 'to conspire' is derived from a Latin word meaning 'to breath together' suggests that this is something that's been recognised for a long time.

Although breathing may seem the most difficult when you first try matching, it can also be the most powerful. Unless some physical or mental cause interferes with our breathing, we don't generally think consciously about it. Rather than staring blatantly at a persons' chest, you can gain a sense of their breathing rate by the speed of their speech, or by the rise and fall of their shoulders that allows you to pace them in their breathing.

All the suggestions for creating rapport by matching in the foregoing involve changes at a behavioural level, and when you experiment moving in a different way or changing your speech patterns it can feel awkward and strange. James Flaherty explains that we all have habits of behaviour, which include how we act, move, talk, think, and respond. They are embedded into our body, into our neuromuscular system:

> 'It is as if through repetition, we've worn grooves into our body making it easy for us to repeat what's happened before and quite challenging to begin new behaviour.'[17]

But the important factor is the starting point. Training yourself to notice the fine detail of the way other people speak and behave shifts the emphasis from self-absorption to broaden your understanding of other people. Genie Laborde writes that external matching accentuates similarities and plays down differences so that understanding and rapport between people can increase. It is a subtle process because none of the techniques should ever be noticed.[18] Making adjustments to your own habits moves you towards other people's experience of themselves. And it is this shift of attention that is crucial to the second important skill in building relationships – listening.

Practice Point 6

Task yourself daily with setting out to notice more about other people and experimenting in how you can match their behaviour.

Day One: you could check out the fine detail of body language: notice how people sit or stand, how they use gestures. Pick one aspect to match with another person, and notice how that feels for you.

Day Two: notice more about how a person's voice sounds. Is their speech deep, slow, resonant, or high pitched, fast, staccato? Test out how you can match the way their voice sounds without sounding artificial. Check out how it feels to do that.

Day Three: see if you can notice patterns in the way people use words. Can you respond in the same style of language?

Can you keep your attention on the *content* of a conversation, while at the same time checking out aspects of the *process?*

The skills of relationship management – Active listening

Primary school teacher Emma has often said to me she feels her Head doesn't really listen to her, but wears a mask of sincerity. 'He puts on this look that he thinks shows he's interested, but I know he's not really'.

Emma's Head is an example of a leader who believes they have become expert at the appearance of communication. And you will probably had a similar experience with someone who may think they're listening, but who you can intuitively sense is really only hearing your words.

For Emma, the effect is demoralising. She feels the Head doesn't really value what she has to say. The result is she feels she doesn't want to bother with putting forward her opinion. Other people I've known have reacted differently to similar examples of poor listening. A college manager used to get quite irate when she sensed the Principal wasn't listening to the ideas she was putting forward. He came across as merely allowing her to speak, with a look on his face that seemed to be saying 'I'm listening to you but I'm not paying you any attention'. In desperation, she would repeat herself over and over in frustrated attempts to gain a response.

I've not yet gone into an organization where people have the ability to listen. Generally people are very bad a listening.

Paul, Consultant on complexity theory and leadership

I've written at length elsewhere on the skills of active listening.[19] The main point to make here is that – just as with creating rapport – real listening is an *active* rather than a *passive* process. As James Flaherty puts it, it's not merely the engagement of the ear and the auditory nerve, it's full engagement of attention to another person.[20] It's not only hearing what's being said, but picking up what's unspoken as well. It's noticing whether another person's body language is consistent with their verbal message, or whether there's a mismatch that suggests a need to test out what's being said. It's making a shift out of a habit of *affecting* listening, while being mentally engaged in thinking about what you're going to say next – probably as soon as you get the opportunity.

As the examples above demonstrate, at an individual level bad listening can damage relationships. Not only that, habits of poor listening can limit the effectiveness of groupwork and meetings. Many meetings involve people talking one after another with little account taken of what earlier speakers have said. Meetings can become individual expressions of opinion rather than the development of ideas by building on what others have been saying.

Good listening, on the other hand, can reap rewards far beyond the exchange of information. At an individual level, it can build on rapport and contribute to the self-esteem of another person. A creative leader will also role model good listening in teams by highlighting points that people are making and encouraging others to develop them, e.g. 'That's an interesting point, John. Stella, from your perspective, would you add anything to that?'

One person had one of the highest sickness levels in college. Working in partnership with personnel and the individual we have turned them around. They had been underperforming for a long while because they were misunderstood and not listened to by previous management. This led to a severe condition that affected both physical and mental well-being. This has now been resolved and the person is performing to an outstanding level and is enjoying work once again. Another was disengaged – obstructive but under-performing. I spent time getting to know them and picked up on an external interest of theirs and gave them the opportunity to put their head above the parapet and take a leading role with colleagues. I started a pilot programme and gave them responsibility for coordinating it. They have come alive.

Maria – College faculty manager

Feedback – Nourishment not punishment

Everyone needs feedback if they are to grow and develop personally and professionally. It's accepted that people new to the teaching profession will need feedback on their performance. Yet as people develop into more senior professional roles, they can become less open to receiving feedback on their leadership. There may be a presumption from people in more junior roles that it's not their place to give feedback. And it maybe that a lack of receptiveness and openness on the part of the leader does not encourage feedback that could enhance their performance.

Of course we all receive feedback in the form of the response of other people to what we say and do. Given a level of *response-ability* featured in the previous chapter, and a raised level of attending to others featured above, a leader should be picking up signals that indicate the acceptability of their words or action. But the danger lies in glossing over reactions from people that could be construed as negative: convinced of the rightness of one's own position, it's easy to fall into the trap of ignoring feedback that says otherwise.

Yet everyone benefits from having 'critical friends'. As this concept has grown in popularity it's become acknowledged as an important function of a board of governors. A board of governors and a Principal or Head will have shared outcomes, making a solid basis for the marrying of unconditional support with critique that is the essence of critical friendship.

The 'loneliness' of a leadership position is a thing of the past. It's recognized now that leaders cannot succeed on their own: even the most outwardly confident executives need support and advice.[21] Working from shared values with colleagues throughout the organisation provides a basis for a supportive and constructive dialogue. Bill George writes that authentic leaders build extraordinary support teams to help them stay on course:

'These teams counsel them in times of uncertainty, help them in times of difficulty, and celebrate with them in times of success... Authentic leaders find that their support teams provide affirmation, advice, perspective, and calls for course corrections when needed.'[22]

Leaders need support networks. They have to have the ability to say 'I don't know what to do: what do you think?'

Paul – Consultant on complexity theory and leadership

Leaders get so much strength from the team. I gain strength for my leadership.

Mal – Secondary School Head

Feedback is necessary to develop self-awareness, and self-awareness also involves being alert to self-denial. The real benefits from feedback come when a leader can be open and honest enough not only to act on critical feedback, and to actively seek the views of colleagues and others in order to enhance their performance, as Bill George and his colleagues have indicated:

'Denial can be the greatest hurdle that leaders face in becoming self-aware. They all have egos that need to be stroked, insecurities that need to be smoothed, fears that need to be allayed. Authentic leaders realize that they have to be willing to listen to feedback – especially the kind they don't want to hear.'[23]

Self-awareness applies as much to giving feedback as to receiving it. There needs to be honesty over the reason to say something: if it's really about inflating your own worth or feeding some need of your own, then it's unlikely to achieve the intended outcome. There's also the potential for the other person to feel resentful and unfairly treated. Rather, following some simple principles, even the most challenging feedback on performance can be made acceptable, and likely to be acted upon.

Constructive feedback deals with behaviour, rather than the person, describing the behaviour rather than making a judgement on it. It needs to be specific, rather than woolly, focusing on the behaviour the person has control over and is able to improve. By demonstrating their own preparedness to accept constructive feedback, and role-modelling empathic feedback behaviour, leaders create an ethos where feedback from colleagues becomes an accepted part of continuous professional development.

Creative leaders influence and encourage feedback by demonstrating in their behaviour that its function is Nourishment not Punishment. In both formal appraisal situations, and informally, the Feedback Sandwich[24] acts as a useful reminder of a formula around which to construct feedback to develop performance. **Practice Point** 7 gives an example of how it can be used to frame informal conversations: in this case after a member of staff had taken an open school assembly for the first time.

Practice Point 7

The Feedback Sandwich

Top Layer	Refer to something specific that has been genuinely well done: *'I really liked the way you made a point of mentioning the success of the school football team'.*
Filling	Refer to some aspect of performance the person can improve: *'Welcoming the parents is always appreciated. You phrased it very warmly, and if you look up and make eye contact with them, that makes the welcome even more sincere'.* (N.B. Too much filling is difficult to swallow. Too spicy and indigestible a filling can cause upset. Reasonable bites can be swallowed and digested)
Bottom Layer	Give a general positive comment: *'Overall, I thought you engaged everyone well'.*

One person I didn't trust and I had a sharp word with her and listed a whole lot of stuff. She was very taken aback. I learnt I should have drip-fed the criticisms, giving regular feedback. It took a couple of years for her to come round and in the end she was one of the stars.

Gloria – HM inspector

> *Leadership is both socially complex and personal. I don't believe in leaders being born – everyone has qualities that can be drawn out. Part of those qualities will be that they can bring out the leadership qualities in others.*
>
> David – Director of Institute of Applied Education Research

Changing relationships

This chapter started with a mention that teachers can no longer depend upon traditional authority, but that the emphasis has shifted to a reliance on the development of professional skills. Just as the experience of an individual teacher has changed, at the same time, models of leadership have also been evolving.

During the 1990s, *collegiality* became enshrined in the folklore of management as the most appropriate way to run schools and colleges. It assumed a common set of values held by members of the organization, and that decisions would be reached by consensus rather division or conflict. The role of the Head or Principal was envisaged as the facilitator of an essentially participative process.[25]

Collegiality became 'the official model of good practice' closely associated with school effectiveness and school improvement. Yet Tony Bush describes it as an ideal type rather than a model founded firmly in practice. The participative nature of consensus may appeal, but in reality the process can be slow and cumbersome. It is probably rare that a 'pure' collegial model could operate within the hierarchical structure of state education, given the Head's ultimate formal accountability to external bodies. Eric Hoyle in particular had argued that bureaucratic and political realities meant that collegiality did not exist in schools.[26]

Fast forward a decade or more, and a new model is being advocated – that of *distributed* leadership. At least it's not yet clear whether it's a new understanding of leadership or a re-working of earlier models such as collegiality. In a review of research on distributed leadership, Nigel Bennett and his colleagues concluded that, if distributed leadership was to be distinctive from other forms of leadership, it would be by means of a concept of leadership as an *emergent property of a group or network of interacting individuals*. The most distinctive feature of distributed leadership would be the additional dynamic as a product of joined activity, i.e. 'where people work together in such a way that they pool their initiative and expertise, the outcome is a product or energy which is greater than the sum of their individual actions'.[27]

And in respect of relationships, distributed leadership would seem to require a re-working of attitudes and behaviours from the perspective of both the person in the leadership 'role' and others to whom 'leadership' is deemed to be distributed.

The skills featured in this chapter are an introduction to relationship-building behavioural techniques that could ensure an authentic model of distributed leadership. Behavioural techniques are only effective within a framework of genuine empathy, derived from core values relating to the basis of human relationships. If distributed leadership is to offer more than mere delegation, we may need to broaden our understanding from more conventional views of leadership.[28] For Alma Harris, relationships are core to creative leadership:

> '...creative leadership is fundamentally about connecting people, often very different people. Creative leadership requires the time, resources, opportunities and space so that mutual learning can occur. The end result, however, is not cosy consensus or comfortable agreement but disagreement, dialogue and creative dissonance. Creative thinking is neither easy nor comfortable; it requires the abandonment of previous thinking and the confronting of established beliefs, mindsets and patterns.'[29]

The behavioural level of practising skills will therefore only be one level of building relationships. Behaviours may need to be grounded in a re-framing of attitudes: attitudes that can provide an equitable basis for a genuinely distributed leadership; a basis from which the behaviour of a creative leader can stimulate the motivation to release the creative capacity of everyone.

CREATIVE LEADERSHIP THINKING SPACE

For a creative leader, development in the area of Relationships can be recognised at different levels. There will be the level of Behaviour and Capability, involving thinking about:

- What are the behavioural strategies I need to practice to maintain productive leadership relationships?

- What are the capabilities that will enable me to nurture and encourage intrinsic motivation in others?

Then at the level of attitudes, thinking about:

- What are the Values and Beliefs that need to underpin the productive relationships and the development of others as creative leaders?

Finally, thinking about yourself, and how you may develop as a result of changes in your behaviour and attitudes:

- How will my view of myself, my Identity as a leader, need to change in light of evolving notions of leadership?

Notes

1 Joseph O'Connor 1998:5
2 Neil Dempster 2009:22
3 From a presentation by David Nicholl, Head of the Northern Ireland Office of the Chartered Institute of Public Finance and Accountancy (CIPFA)
4 Julian Elliot et al. 2011:84
5 *Ibid.* 2011:99
6 *Ibid.* 2011:99–100
7 Daniel Goleman 2002:51
8 *Ibid.* 2002:48–9
9 I've given a fuller account of Rachael's experience elsewhere, see Jacquie Turnbull 2007:113–14
10 Daniel Goleman 2002:51
11 Sue Knight 1995:123
12 Professor Tim Brighouse, Wales Education Lecture 2005
13 Joseph O'Connor 1998:81
14 Genie Z. Laborde 1998:36
15 Daniel Goleman 2002:2
16 David Wood 1998:29
17 James Flaherty 2005:100
18 Genie Z. Laborde 1998:33
19 See Chapter 6: Attentive Listening, Jacquie Turnbull 2007:117–32, 2nd Edition, forthcoming.
20 James Flaherty 2005:55
21 Bill George et al. 2007:136
22 *Ibid.* 2007:136
23 *Ibid.* 2007:134

24 Model of feedback reproduced from their training materials with permission from Stenhouse Consulting

25 Tony Bush 1997:68–79

26 Eric Hoyle 1986:100

27 Nigel Bennett et al. 2003:7

28 Alma Harris 2009:5

29 *Ibid.* 2008:11

9

Grow: Personal Qualities

The fast pace of change in our modern world means we all have to engage in lifelong learning. Creative leaders need to understand our modern world, and work with its complexity. To do this, they need to be able to respond flexibly to the needs of different people, to be adaptable to different situations, to manage their own emotions and feelings. This chapter draws together attitudes that have been implicit throughout the book and defines their influence on personal development. As with the skills of Relationships, they are attitudes that can be learned. They are essential elements that allow a person to Grow both as a person and as a creative leader. For as Peter Senge has written, if you want to be a leader, you have to be a real human being: you must understand yourself first.[1]

The starting point for this book as been the changing nature of life and work in the twenty-first century. The implications of living in a fast-changing world cannot be ignored; either in respect of how educators can best prepare young people for their future, or from the perspective of the professional development of educators themselves.

The nature of the changes mean that, more than ever before, traditional academic qualifications and training are not the only yardstick by which people will demonstrate their effectiveness in employment. In Chapter 1 the quote from Daniel Goleman makes it plain that the 'new rules' relate to how well we handle ourselves and each other.

The rules mean that we need to be more aware than ever before of the link between personal development and professional effectiveness.

Research into the top performing school systems that informed the influential McKinsey Report found that only a small handful of personal traits explained a high proportion of the variation in leadership effectiveness.[2] In this respect, we can probably conclude that the attributes of leadership are closely aligned to the attributes of being an authentic, creative human being, skilled in self-management and relationships. Warren Bennis and Joan Goldsmsith describe it thus:

> '...the process of becoming a leader is much the same as the process of becoming an integrated human being...leadership is a metaphor for centeredness, congruity and balance in one's life.'[3]

The importance of these attributes are especially emphasized in education, given that leadership by its nature influences, inspires and motivates 'followers', and the stakeholders of a school or college will include young people, parents and the local community, as well as colleagues. There is what's been called the 'moral imperative' of the leader modelling the value principles of a school or college into practice.[4] But additionally, the leaders' capacity to demonstrate personal effectiveness as well as professional competence has the potential to influence young people of the credibility of authentic and congruent personal behaviour.

There's an overarching aspect that links all the sections that follow in this chapter. It was indicated when the 75 members of Stanford Graduate School of Business's Advisory Council were asked to recommend the most important capability for leaders to develop. Their answer was nearly unanimous: *self-awareness*.[5] Their response echoes the relevant importance of the three strands of emotional intelligence featured in Chapter 8: self-awareness, self-management and empathy.[6] Plainly, understanding yourself underpins all development towards authentic and creative leadership.

Leadership is not different from your natural personality. You learn to temper it and you do that with your leadership as well.

Gordon – Research and Consultancy Director

You have to be the leader you are.

Mal – Secondary School Head

Learning for life

Your self-awareness includes how much you think you know. Michael Fullan warns about the danger of knowing a lot as a leader, because the more you know, the more you want to control. It's hard to avoid overmanaging when you know a lot as a leader. But the point is, leaders who thrive and survive are people who know they don't know everything.[7]

It's about balancing any urge to be controlling because of what you know, with a recognition that you need to be constantly learning. I once worked with a Principal who thought he had to demonstrate he knew everything. He thought to acknowledge there were things he had yet to learn would be a sign of weakness, so his mind was closed to what might have been helpful advice. Because he thought he knew best he wore himself out trying to be all things to all people. When there was a staff training event in college he insisted on presenting the whole content himself and taking control of every detail of the arrangements. The consequence was no sense of involvement or purpose for the staff and many simply switched off.

Robert Sternberg writes that creative leaders realise that they never know enough, and are constantly expanding their knowledge base and horizons, regardless of their age. He gives the example of Nelson Mandela as one of the best examples of a lifelong learner. The experience of spending much of a life in prison might have led to him becoming bitter, vengeful, even unbalanced, but instead he went on to become one of the great leaders of the twentieth century.[8]

A leader's attitude to learning is encapsulated in their own openness and interest; in retaining the 'innocence of eye' of childhood.[9] Stephen Fry thinks inquisitiveness is one of the greatest human instincts there is: it is the hunger that allows us to fuel ourselves with knowledge, understanding, insight and confidence.[10]

This element of inquisitiveness is not be equated with 'nosiness' of course. Rather it's the openness to seeing even the familiar as fresh and new. Making the familiar strange was advocated in Chapter 8 – turning a fresh eye to what others say and do in order to develop relationships. Peter Senge thinks it's the indicator of natural leaders that they commit a lifetime of effort to developing conceptual and communication skills, reflecting on personal values, learning how to listen and to appreciate others and their ideas: 'In the absence of such effort, personal charisma is style without substance'.[11]

I have a high degree of self-doubt, which I think is good because if you're convinced you're right you'll not always make the right decision. With self-

> *doubt you're more likely to listen properly to people and therefore more likely to make a better decision.*
>
> Janet – Primary School Teacher
>
> *Foolish leaders think they've got all the answers.*
>
> Gloria – HM inspector

Being involved in education, of course, means that an attitude of lifelong learning not only enhances a leaders' personal development, but also influences others by example. Despite an emergent international focus on a need for lifelong learning to enable people to cope with the complexity of a global knowledge society, many young people still think their 'learning' ends along with their schooling. I have spoken to employers who speak ruefully of graduates who believe they bring all the knowledge and skills needed to fulfil a role in industry or business. And regrettably the experience of meeting experienced teachers who exhibit an attitude of having nothing left to learn has been repeated more than once.

So a leaders' role in this respect is crucial. A leaders' attitude to learning influences the creation of a learning culture that encompasses staff as well as students, and extends its influence to governors, parents and stakeholders. Part of this attitude will be the leader's interpretation of their role in nurturing the learning of others. McKinsey reported that the systems which seek to use their Principals as drivers of reform expect them to be excellent instructors who spent most of their time coaching teachers. One successful Principal interviewed described his role thus:

> 'Being a teacher is about helping children to learn. Being a principal is about helping adults to learn. That's why it's tough...I walk the halls, I walk the halls, I walk the halls...I only look at my inbox once everybody leaves.'[12]

Taking learning as a focus encourages a climate of continuous professional development for everyone. Being open and inclusive about learning encourages teachers to feel confident about sharing expertise and feedback and regularly observing each others practice. Stimulating a culture that recognizes everyone as learners can break down silo mentalities that can restrict learning to subject expertise. One college actively supported faculty staff in studying for masters degrees in educational management. The Principal extended this encouragement to the college finance officers because he wanted them to broaden their knowledge and understanding and engage in the educational mission of the college.

This universal encouragement requires a relentless enthusiasm for learning. A leader's enthusiasm and own motivation can provide the energy to engage everyone in learning and development. As Howard Gardner and his colleagues describe, it is a mark of a creative person:

'Creative people are usually driven by curiosity and tend to be more intrinsically motivated – more interested in the rewards of intellectual discovery than in financial or status rewards. Therefore, they are often considered odd both by the general public and by fellow practitioners. But the reason innovators are less concerned with money and power is that they get their reward directly from their work. They are satisfied by the excitement and wonder involved in the process of discovery – a fulfilment no amount of money can buy'.[13]

Trustworthiness

Openness to learning is not the only feature that encourages an environment where the learning of everyone can be nurtured. Neil Dempster and George Bagakis claim that the environment needs to be safe and secure if learning for all is the goal. Crucial to this is that a climate of trust must exist – between the leader and teachers, between teachers and teaching assistants, between teachers and parents.[14]

Like rapport featured in Chapter Eight, trust doesn't just happen by luck or mutual understanding; for Robert Solomon and Fernando Flores it's something that can be cultivated by skill and commitment. Although trust may often seem invisible – or transparent – it is the result of continuous attentiveness, activity and change. Put simply, telling the truth establishes trust and lying destroys it. Trust is also described as emotion: trusting people – like loving them – not only appreciates and depends upon other people, it *changes* them, and usually for the better.[15]

Being a 'real' person is essential for establishing trust. Coming across to others as a real person is not just about openness about ourselves, it also entails a consistency between what we say and what we do. We will all have had an experience of someone saying something, but intuitively feeling they didn't mean it. It may not be something we would put into words, but it's enough to create a feeling of *dis*trust that can impair a relationship. Daniel Goleman suggests credibility stems from integrity: and integrity – acting openly, honestly and consistently – sets apart outstanding performers in jobs of every kind.[16]

The issue in relating trust to creativity is that creativity and innovation can involve risk. Without a climate of trust, people are not likely to put forward ideas or experiment for fear of failure. Trust is maintained through the honest sharing of information and is at its best when failures are openly discussed.[17] The change that trust can stimulate can be the confidence to take initiatives, to allow people to grow into their own leadership abilities. For Thomas Sergiovanni, the building of trust is not just an interpersonal aspect, but is an organisational quality:

> Once embedded in the culture of the school, trust works to liberate people to be their best, to give others their best, and to take risks.[18]

Practice Point 8

Honest feedback from others on how they perceive you is essential to enable you to Grow as a leader. As a professional trainer I depended upon the insight gained from delegates completing an evaluation at the end of a course. This would ask for a response to statements about the content of the course, and the quality of the materials, but also about the approachability, professionalism and knowledge of myself as a trainer. Such 360 degree feedback has become popularised in business as a method for gathering a 'full circle' of assessments, e.g. from subordinates, peers, line managers, and sometimes customers or clients.

These strategies can be useful in relation to issues such as trustworthiness or empathy, where it may be difficult to gain open and honest feedback on a personal level. Whatever strategy you use, it should include certain important elements to encourage objective responses on how others perceive you, and ensure you gain the most from the experience:

- It allows the response to be anonymous
- It uses a method such as numbering
- It describes the *behaviours* of the attitudes you want to test
- You respect the results as expressions of how your colleagues perceive you
- You are prepared to use the feedback to help you Grow as a leader

Depending upon which aspect of your personal development you want to improve, you could adapt the example below to gain an assessment from your colleagues. And you may also find it useful to compare their responses with your own assessment of your attitudes.

Table 5 – Assessment

	Never	Seldom	Sometimes	Often	Always
In relations with others, I show sensitivity to their needs	1	2	3	4	5
I seek to develop the potential of others	1	2	3	4	5
I show a tolerance of differences in people	1	2	3	4	5
I show a willingness to experiment with ideas from others	1	2	3	4	5
I am attentive in listening to others	1	2	3	4	5
I express honest feelings and attitudes about myself to others	1	2	3	4	5
I am concerned to improve the performance of others	1	2	3	4	5

I knew one person who had read all the books, knew 'the speak', could portray themselves as a good leader, but when the pressure was on, the true person came out. They could quote the values but didn't live them at all.

Kay – Faculty Manager

As long as you're consistent staff can cope. But if you're everyone's friend one day and a barking tyrant the next people don't know where they are.

Mal – Secondary Headteacher

With creativity comes acceptance that things will go wrong.

Gordon – Director, research and consultancy company

Creative thinking

Sadly the early curiosity of childhood often withers through the effects of ageing and schooling. Deputy Headteacher Peter Hyman is not the only one who thinks the education system is not designed to get children to think.[19] Even young children can recognise the truth of that from their experience: as one child said to Robert Fisher, 'I like school. You don't have to think. They tell you what to do'.[20]

If this is the experience of childhood, perhaps it's not surprising that as adults we may feel ill-equipped for creative thinking. Both the emphasis on rational and logical thinking throughout schooling, and the rational orientation of management does not provide a fertile seed-bed for creative thinking. Yet John Adair claims, even if your work in the narrow sense does not call for imagination, the art of creative thinking is still relevant. It's not what happens to you in life that matters, but how you respond, and the creative response is to transform bad things into good, problems into opportunities.[21]

Creative thinking is not necessarily imaginative thinking. New ideas are not formed out of nothing; creative thinking starts with what already exists, the creative mind sees possibilities in them or connections that are invisible to less creative minds. And creative thinking often involves a leap in the dark.[22] In Chapter 6 you saw how Siriol made links between different events and information to create an initiative to develop emotional literacy and boost the self-confidence and self-esteem of young people. And in Chapter Five there was the example of Denise who connected government policy with the concerns of local youth workers and the mission of her college governors, who involved colleagues in different departments of her college, and who inspired lecturers in her department to create an innovative course that addressed the specific needs of vulnerable young people.

What these examples also demonstrate is that having good ideas is not the whole answer to problematic issues. A creative leader also has the skills to persuade others to listen to their ideas.[23] Without the basis of good rapport featured in Chapter 8, creative leaders would not be able to convince others of the value of their ideas. Without openness and active listening, a leader will not be alert to making the links that culminate in creative action.

'Chance favours the prepared mind'

I believe it was Paul McCarthy who said the lyrics of one of the Beatles songs came to him in a dream. Not as strange as it may seem really – you've probably at some stage followed advice to 'sleep on it' to find the solution to a problem. And it's something that can occur involuntarily as well.

You may be the sort of person who relies upon the strident call of an alarm to raise you from a deep slumber. But I'm sure there are other times when you press the snooze button to allow yourself the luxury of waking slowly. It's in that space between deep sleep and full wakefulness that inspiration often seems to occur. For me, it can be the next stage of something I'm writing. A whole paragraph may come into my mind, almost ready written, so that I have to get up quickly, and switch on the computer to capture it before it's lost. Another time it may be the solution to a problem I'd previously been grappling with: it will occur, seemingly out of nowhere, apparently without any conscious thought on my part.

The fact that creative ideas can occur, as with Paul McCarthy, seemingly in a dream, gives a clue to how to influence creative thinking. New ideas do not necessarily result from the application hard conscious thinking. In fact, the reverse is more likely. Where was Archimedes when the insight into a theory of displacement occurred to him? Having a relaxing bath of course. Did Newton come upon a theory of gravity when pouring over mathematical formulae at his desk? No, he was sat in an orchard taking in the pleasures of nature.

Even so, momentous historical discoveries do not occur out of nowhere. What Archimedes and Newton had in common was the hard graft they had put in ahead of the moment they latched upon their new theory. With the hard work done, an everyday occurrence then enabled them to make a connection that provided the last piece of the jigsaw. Just as a painter or sculptor will take a step back to take a different perspective on their work, they needed the moment when two elements came together: first, they had done the preparation so were open and receptive to a new angle, and secondly the new idea occurred when they were relaxed and not necessarily consciously thinking about the problem.

The examples of Archimedes and Newton have been handed down to us as examples of how original ideas came into being. But it's not just a process that occurs with great original thinkers. It's a process we can all use in developing creative thinking. I've always advised students not to burn the midnight oil grappling to find the words for an essay or assignment, particularly in relation to the final paragraph or conclusion. Rather, I'd say, leave it overnight and in the morning the words will be there for you. I don't think my advice was often taken; even reassuring them with, 'trust me, I'm a teacher', they were still inclined to look rather sceptical.

Leaving aside the tendency of students to leave assignments to the last minute, there's also a common perception that 'thinking' demands hard conscious effort. But the truth is our brains have significantly more capacity than is revealed in our conscious thinking. The complexity of the average brain is quite difficult to comprehend in numbers: a hundred billion neurons (brain cells) connected by a hundred trillion synapses (the gaps where electrical impulses pass between cells).[24] So the capacity is there to enable us to develop creative thinking. We just have to trust the process.

John Adair advises that knowing when to turn away from a problem and leave it for a while is an essential skill in the art of creative thinking. We need to resist the temptation of worrying at a problem like a dog with a bone, and hand the problem over to what he terms our 'Depth Mind'. It doesn't matter that we don't know exactly how sleep and relaxation work in synthesising patterns of thought into creative solutions: what matters is that it works.

When I was at college, as students we used to joke about 'distractor' activities; how we would do *anything* rather than get down to writing an essay. I'm not a lover of household chores but I could always find a piece of furniture that needed dusting or a toilet that needed cleaning rather than engaging in the more difficult work of thinking. One friend said she had the best groomed cat in the neighbourhood because of the number of times she turned to the task to avoid having to engage in serious thinking. Nowadays I suppose the technological attractions of social networking and gameplaying will be the biggest draw for the procrastinating students.

We probably all indulge in delaying tactics in some form or another to avoid the pain of having to formulate a difficult decision. But actually, used with discipline, this is a process that can work for you. The proviso must be that you have all the information you need, but then 'switching off' from wrestling with an issue and turning to some mundane activity allows your unconscious mind to synthesise the information. Many writers take a daily walk as part of their routine for just that purpose. In relation to 'sleeping on it' John Adair advocates actively influencing the process by programming your Depth Mind with the information for a few minutes before going to sleep, in anticipation of the 'print-out' of the solution when you wake.[25]

Practice Point 9

- Integrate into your working life daily opportunities to allow your creative unconscious free rein. Take a break rather than continuing to grapple with a problem: mentally put it to one side, switch to a mundane task that allows you to go on automatic pilot, physically walk away from it. Be honest that you're not just ignoring the problem: rather fix the time when you'll be coming back to it with your creative mind refreshed.

- Recognize when discussions at team meeting have become tautological arguments. Learn to recognize the crucial difference between going round in circles and building ideas into creative solutions. If it's the former, capture where you are on a flip chart and draw a line under the discussion. Depending on the urgency of the issue, return to it at the end of the meeting, or at a later time.
- Develop trust in your creative mind and allow yourself to 'sleep on it'. Think of the issue you want to work on before you go to bed, then clear your mind for sleep. Model Barry Gibb of the Bee Gees who keeps a tape recorder beside his bed to capture a new tune in his mind when he wakes. Have a recorder or notebook handy to keep hold of your first thoughts when you wake.

Emotional intelligence

Another theme of this book has been that IQ ratings and qualifications as defined in traditional schooling are no longer sufficient to ensure survival or success of young people in our modern world. But Daniel Goleman points to a dangerous paradox at work: as children grow ever smarter in IQ, their emotional intelligence (EI) is on the decline.[26] You saw in Chapter 4 that there has been a sharp decline in the emotional health of young people over the past 25 years, and Goleman cites a survey that demonstrates there has been a steady worsening of children's emotional intelligence.

While this doesn't bode well for young people themselves, it is even more significant for future leaders since the competencies of EI are being seen as defining features of highly effective leadership in other sectors.[27] From a survey of 40 companies to define what set star performers apart from average performers, emotional competencies proved *twice* as important in contributing to excellence as were pure intellect and expertise.[28] Unsurprisingly then, there has been a growing interest in EI in all sectors of education, amongst both practitioners and policy makers alike. It's significant that a policy document advocating building distributed leadership and expertise throughout a school system, placed EI first amongst recommended attributes:

'Leadership needs to be emotionally intelligent, purposeful, enabling, influencing, motivating and focused on building the skills, knowledge and personal attributes of all those involved in the structure.'[29]

Generally, the idea that certain skills and competencies are needed for the work of building relationships has found expression in the concept of EI. Even though there has been a long recognition that teaching requires a degree of empathy and awareness of others, there has been a significant shift in attitudes. The recognition that EI can enhance learning can be detected in the introduction of programmes for children and young people. And, significantly for us, a capacity for EI is also claimed to predict outstanding leadership performance.[30]

Aspects of the leadership competencies of EI have been implicit in what's been covered already: *Social Awareness* has been featured in the importance of empathy, and the need to understand the politics and organisation of schooling; *Relationship Management* has been illustrated in the cultivation and maintenance of relationships; *Self-Awareness* has been related to a need for self-assessment of learning. The fourth domain of emotional intelligence – *Self-Management* – can be detected in an authentic openness to receive feedback from others, and will be evident in an ability to be flexible and adaptable.[31]

Adaptability

Daniel Goleman describes adaptability as the ability to juggle multiple demands without losing focus or energy, and the capacity for leaders to be comfortable with the ambiguities of organisational life.[32] This is a capability that has been a key theme of Part 1 of this book. Each chapter in Part One featured tensions and ambiguities in education with which a creative leader had to perform a 'balancing act': change v. stability, professionalism v. task orientation, time control v. autonomy, finding a balance in relation to the purpose of education.

The reason for featuring the tensions and ambiguities in Part One is that they cannot be ignored; creative decision-making may be necessary to resolve them. The issue of the purpose of education for example, will be for each leader and organization to define in relation to their priorities. Rather than giving in to the temptation to avoid the discomfort of such ambiguities, Robert Sternberg recognizes that creative leaders tolerate the ambiguity long enough to ensure that they make a correct decision.[33]

For the leaders featured in this book, their values act as a key stabilising force that enable them to handle conflicting pressures. Clarity about values needs to come first, then integration of personal values with values for the organization to achieve a values consensus. A values-driven organisation not only has a benchmark for decision-making, the values provide a stabilising force that resists the buffeting of conflicting demands, allowing leaders to keep them in perspective while focusing on consistent and congruent decision-making.

Some of the conflicting demands may entail pressure to conform – you have also seen in Part 1 how the structure and system of schooling has proved remarkably resistant to change. Adaptability by taking creative action may not always be appreciated if the actions are surprising or even risky. A creative leader may need *ego-strength* to withstand pressure to conform or to forego original ideas in favour of more conventional action.[34]

Most of the time I'm driven by their collective wisdom, but I have to take the decision. This is the bravery leaders have to have.

Mal – Headteacher

Robert Sternberg also features adaptability in his synthesis of the elements of educational leadership. He interprets these in a particular way: by adding *wisdom* to complete a model that includes intelligence and creativity:

'Wise leaders do not look out just for their own interest, nor do they ignore these interests. Rather, they skilfully balance interests of varying kinds, including their own, those of their followers, and those of the organization for which they are responsible…Leaders can be intelligent in various ways and creative in various ways; it does not guarantee they are particularly wise.'[35]

Robert Sternberg recognises that educational leaders are continually facing decisions whether to take risks or fall back on the tried and (not always) true. This element of wisdom in creative leadership will influence a knowledge of when to take risks and when not to and particularly, what risks are worth taking.[36]

For these writers then, *ego-strength* and *wisdom* are attributes that enable leaders to take decisions while balancing multiple pressures and interests. And being able to achieve this balancing act over a sustained period of time requires a further attribute developed below.

Tenacity

People who are high achievers in their field can exhibit extraordinary levels of perseverance in sticking with their aims. Tennis ace Jimmy Connors was once losing a match 6–1, 6–1, 4–1 before going on to win. Defeat just wasn't an option.

Many scientific and technological developments that we take for granted would not have been available to us without years of dedicated research and development. James Dyson developed 5,127 prototypes over five years before producing the world's first bagless vacuum cleaner.

You also saw in Chapter 2 that James had tenaciously pursued his dream to become a top chef, enduring financial hardship and excessively long working hours in the process.

What is it that allows people to maintain almost superhuman effort, sometimes over a long period of time, to achieve a goal that is deemed to be personally worthwhile? *Self-efficacy*, *personal mastery* and *agency* are all terms that relate to this sort of ability to be able to pursue valued goals, and belief about personal capabilities is a strong determinant in this respect. Albert Bandura's research has consistently demonstrated that efficacy beliefs have a significant influence on motivation and attainment:[37]

> 'People with high assurance in their capabilities in given domains approach difficult tasks as challenges to be mastered rather than as threats to be avoided...These people set themselves challenging goals and maintain strong commitment to them. They heighten and sustain their efforts in the face of difficulties. They quickly recover their sense of efficacy after failures or setbacks. They attribute failure to insufficient effort or to deficient knowledge and skills that are acquirable. They approach threatening situations with assurance that they can exercise control over them.'[38]

The *self-belief* that underpins *self-efficacy* is rather more than just acknowledging a particular capability. Albert Bandura points out that saying one is capable should not be confused with believing it to be so, and is not necessarily self-convincing. Self-efficacy beliefs come about from a complex process of integrating personal knowledge, feedback and experience, and once formed are a significant determinant of the level and quality of achievement.[39]

So self-belief is not the same as a strongly held view whereby someone can dogmatically pursue a course of action, ignoring evidence to the contrary. Rather, the self-belief that underpins self-efficacy is a learning process, what Carol Dweck has described as a 'Growth Mindset'[40], an attitude that depends upon the relationship with learning featured earlier. It's a realism that also provides the other side of the coin to the open and exploratory attitude that creative people bring to problem situations. It's a reference back to the relationship between creativity and discipline in leadership (*see Chapter 5*). And Michael Mumford and his colleagues confirm the exploratory attitude is only half the story:

> '...creative people, while open and curious, will at times, display a harsh evaluative orientation with respect to their own work that that of others'.[41]

Flexibility of style

Many theories of leadership have been based on the issue of style, with styles being categorised generally on a range between autocratic and democratic. The assumption has been that individual leaders will have a way of operating in which they feel most comfortable, which becomes their habitual style.[42]

When it comes to creative leadership, however, it seems sticking with a habitual style is not enough; the more important aspect will be the ability to adopt different styles. You've already seen that Chapter 6 has advocated *response-ability* to changing environments, cultures and climates as a key feature of a creative leader. Roland Bel then suggests a style of leadership also needs to evolve during stages of innovative work. Visionary leadership is necessary at the beginning of an innovation process, then a participative style is needed to get the employees involved, followed by transactional leadership.[43]

This capacity to develop visions through to tangible outcomes does indeed require different ways of thinking and behaving. As a creativity strategy, Robert Dilts suggests no-one embodied this skill more completely than Walt Disney. Disney personified the ability to take his innovative vision through a process of constant improvement and realise a business strategy that established an empire in the field of entertainment. Apparently Disney's team recognised there were three different Walts: the dreamer, the realist and the critic, three processes that link creative ideas to innovative outcomes:

'The dreamer is necessary to form new ideas and goals. The realist is necessary as a means to transform ideas into concrete expressions. The critic is necessary as a filter and as a stimulus for refinement.'[44]

In reality, these roles are often taken by different individuals in a team. Whether the leader enacts these styles personally, or encourages others to contribute the different aspects, depends upon the leader recognizing the importance of each function in the first place. A creative leader may need to shift between the different perspectives in the absence of someone else able to take up that particular style, or if only to demonstrate their individual importance to the passage between ideas and realisation.

'Some Deputy Heads only experience one style of leadership. I've been lucky, I have the opportunities to experience different styles. One was

absolutely outstanding, clear thinking and a huge force. The second was old-fashioned, liked a quiet life. The third wanted to do well but didn't have the dynamism to see good ideas through.'

Mal – Headteacher

The last 20 years I think we've fallen out of love with charismatic and dogmatic leadership. It's also as women have become more influential. Now we look more for balance, judgement, honesty.

Gordon – Research and Consultancy Director

Creative leadership

Some have argued that leaders need not share the expertise and creative problem-solving skills of their followers. Michael Mumford admits these arguments may be plausible, but they are not supported by the available evidence. Rather, the evidence from business contexts indicates that both technical expertise and creative problem-solving skills are essential to lead creative people in order to provide the credibility to exercise influence.[45]

As far as creativity in education is concerned, the argument presented in this book has been that its nurture is crucial to enable young people to develop their potential in a complex and fast-changing society. In relation to the ability to cope with an unknown future, the emphasis is shifting from the value of defined areas of knowledge to the value of thinking and acting creatively. It therefore must follow that, in order to deal with this shift of emphasis, and to prepare young people with the skills and attitudes they will need, educators themselves will need to act creatively.

From the education sector has come evidence that organisations demonstrate success when their leaders act as 'instructional leaders', with principals identifying their main role as supporting and coaching teachers. If we take the example from business above, where both technical expertise **and** creative problem-solving skills are deemed essential to lead creative people, it must follow that this role of 'instructional leader' needs to expand to include role-modelling and nurturing creative thinking and behaviour.

There is every reason why a notion of creativity should be applied to leadership. 'Little c creativity' has been referred to as an 'everyday' creativity evident in high-level problem-solving skills, displayed in productive relationships that generate fresh ideas, demonstrated in human ingenuity in all its forms. We can recognize creativity in leadership by the results leaders achieve by the fact that the organization they lead is uniquely successful in their own field, or when they take a failing organization and transform it into one that achieves unprecedented outcomes.

Creative leaders understand our modern world, and can work with it's complexity. For Robert Sternberg, effective educational leadership involves both skills and attitudes, different types of intelligence, and the flexibility to exhibit them as required:

'A creative leader needs creative skills and attitudes to generate powerful ideas; analytical intelligence to determine whether they are good ideas; practical intelligence to implement the ideas effectively and to persuade others to listen to and follow the ideas; and wisdom to ensure that the ideas represent a common good for all stakeholders, not just for some of them.'[46]

CREATIVE LEADERSHIP THINKING SPACE

The **Grow** theme of this last chapter is perhaps the most crucial of all because it draws together the themes of the whole book. The themes of growth and lifelong learning also encapsulate my personal philosophy which I have attempted to integrate into its pages. In relation to leadership, it is a philosophy that has been summed up neatly by Bill George and his colleagues:

You do not have to be born with specific characteristics or traits of a leader. You do not have to wait for a tap on the shoulder. You do not have to be at the top of your organization. Instead, you can discover your potential right now.[47]

It's because of the philosophy of lifelong learning and growth, that I would prefer not to end this book with a conclusion, but rather to leave you with some questions that relate to the framework for creative leadership: Inspire – Motivate – Grow. I hope they are questions that will provide you with signposts on your journey towards your future as a creative leader in education:

Inspire
- How do you ensure everyone you work with is attuned to the vision for your organisation?

- What do you need to do to help everyone understand their role in fulfilling the vision?

- Are your personal values in tune with the values of the organisation?

- How are your personal values evident in your behaviour: do you 'walk the talk'?

Motivate

- Where and how are you practicing the behavioural strategies to maintain productive leadership relationships?

- How are you developing the capabilities to enable you to nurture and encourage intrinsic motivation in others?

- Do you regularly check the Values and Beliefs that underpin your relationships to ensure they consistent developing others as creative leaders?

Grow

- How does your view of yourself, your Identity as a leader, need to change in light of evolving notions of leadership?

- How are you investing in your personal growth to develop your growth as a leader?

- How are you growing your creative capacity to be more innovative in your leadership?

- How are you developing the creative capacity of young people, of colleagues, within your community?

- What impact will you have as a creative leader in education?

Notes

1 Peter Senge et al. 2004:186
2 Barber, M. & Mourshed, M. 2007:30 ('McKinsey Report')
3 Warren Bennis and Joan Goldsmith 1997:8
4 Richard Churches and John West-Burnham 2008:11
5 Bill George et al. 2007:133
6 Daniel Goleman 2002:51
7 Michael Fullan 2008:126
8 Robert Sternberg 2005:352
9 Dorothea Brande 1996:105
10 Stephen Fry quoted by Katherine Richardson & Jay Allnut 2009

11 Peter Senge 1990:359

12 Barber, M. & Mourshed, M 2007:30–1 ('McKinsey Report')

13 Howard Gardner et al. 2001:20

14 Neil Dempster and George Bagakis 2009:98

15 Robert Solomon and Fernando Flores 2001

16 Daniel Goleman 1996:90

17 Neil Dempster and George Bagakis 2009:99

18 Thomas Sergiovanni 2005:90

19 As quoted by Neil Tweedie 2010:9

20 Robert Fisher 2005:1

21 John Adair 2009:118

22 *Ibid.* 2009:7–8

23 Robert Sternberg 2005:349

24 Stephen Pinker 2002:42

25 John Adair 2009:101–7

26 Daniel Goleman 1998:11

27 Daniel Goleman 2002:38

28 Daniel Goleman 1998:320

29 School Effectiveness Framework, DCELLs, Welsh Assembly Government 2008:12

30 Jocelyn Robson and Bill Bailey 2009:103

31 For a description of Emotional Intelligence Domains and their leadership competencies see Daniel Goleman 2002:253–6

32 Daniel Goleman 2002:252

33 Robert J. Sternberg 2005:351

34 Mark Runco 2004:23

35 Robert Sternberg 2005:358

36 *Ibid.* 2005:350

37 Albert Bandura 1992

38 Albert Bandura 1995:11

39 *Ibid.* 1995:11

40 Carol Dweck 2006

41 Michael Mumford et al. 2002:711

42 Charles Handy 1993:109

43 Roland Bel 2010:56

44 Robert Dilts 1996:87

45 Michael Mumford et al. 2002:712

46 Robert Sternberg 2005:348

47 Bill George et al. 2007:130

References

Abuhamdeh, S. & Csikszentmihalyi, M. (2004) 'The Artistic Personality: A Systems Perspective', in Sternberg, R. J., Grigorenko, E. L., and Singer, J. L. *Creativity: From Potential to Realization*. Washington DC: American Psychological Association.

Adair, J. (2009) *The Art of Creative Thinking: How to be innovative and develop great ideas*. London: Kogan Page Ltd.

Alexander, R. (1997) *Policy and practice in primary education: Local initiative, national agenda* (2nd Edition). London: Routledge.

Apple, M. W. & Beane, J. A. (1999) *Democratic Schools: Lessons from the Chalk face*. Buckingham: Open University Press.

Arkin, A. (2009) 'Back-seat drivers'. *People Management*, 7 May 2009, 26–8.

Arnold, J. & Randall, R. et al. (2010) *Work Psychology: Understanding Human Behaviour in the Workplace* (5th Edition). Harlow, Essex: Pearson Education Ltd.

Asthana, A. (2007) 'Bosses give school reform a failure mark'. *The Observer*, 12 August.

—(2008) 'They don't live for work ... they work to live'. *The Observer*, 25 May.

Atkinson, D. (2004) 'Theorising how student teachers form their identities in initial teacher education', *British Education Research Journal*, 30: 3: 379–94.

Atkinson, W. S. Sir (2009) *Closing the Gap: A response from the chalkface*. The Wales Education Lecture. Cardiff: General Teaching Council for Wales.

Attwood, G., Cross, P. & Hamilton, J. (2003) Re-engaging with education. *Research Papers in Education* 18(1), pp.75–95.

Baggini, J. (2011) 'How Steve Jobs changed capitalism'. *The Guardian*, 6 October 2011.

Bandura, A. (1992) 'Exercise of personal agency through the self-efficacy mechanism', in Schwarzer, R. (ed.) *Self-efficacy: Thought Control of Action*. Washington, DC: Hemisphere, pp.3–38.

Bandura, A. (ed.) (1995) *Self-Efficacy in Changing Societies*. Cambridge: Cambridge University Press.

Barber, M. & Mourshed, M. (2007) How the world's best-performing school systems come out on top. McKinsey & Co.

Barkham, P. (2009) 'A sixth of a GCSE in 60 minutes?' *The Guardian*, 13 February, pp.4–7.

Beadle, P. (2010) *How to Teach*. Carmarthen, Wales: Crown House Publishing Ltd.

Beare, H., Caldwell, B. & Millikan, R. (1997) Dimensions of Leadership in Crawford, M., Kydd, & Riches, C. *Leadership and teams in educational management*. Buckingham: Open University Press, pp.24–39.

Beccalli, N. (2004) When Style Matters in Leadership. European Business Forum Special Report, January 2004. London: European Business Forum.

Bel, R. (2010) Leadership and Innovation: Learning from the Best. *Global Business & Organizational Excellence (USA)* Vol. 29 No. 2, pp.47–61.

Bennett, N., Wise, C., Woods, P. and Harvey, J. A. (2003) Distributed Leadership. Nottingham: National College for School Leadership.

Bennis, W. and Goldsmith, J. (1997) *Learning to Lead.* London: Nicolas Brealey Publishing.

Bernstein, B. (1970) 'Education Cannot Compensate for Society'. *New Society* 15 (387).

Brande, D. (1996) Becoming a Writer. London: Macmillan Reference Books.

Brighouse, T. (2005) 'Teachers: A Comprehensive Success', the Wales Education Lecture. Cardiff: General Teaching Council for Wales.

Burnard, P. & White, J. (2008) 'Creativity and performativity: counterpoints in British and Australian education', *British Education Research Journal* Vol. 34 No. 5, 667–82.

Bush, T. (1997) Collegial models in Harris, A., Bennett, N. & Preedy, M. (eds) *Organizational effectiveness and improvement in education.* Buckingham: Open University Press, pp.68–79.

Carey, J. Churches, R., Hutchinson, G., Jones, J. & Tosey, P. (2010) *Summary Report: Neuro-linguistic programming and learning: Teacher case studies on the impact of NLP in education.* Reading: CfBT Education Trust.

Carlen, J., Gleeson, D. & Wardhaugh, J. (1992) *Truancy: The Politics of Compulsory Schooling.* Buckingham: Open University Press.

Carver, J. (1997) *Board that Make a Difference: A new design for leadership in non-profit and public organizations.* San Francisco CA: John Wiley & Sons Inc.

Caulkin, S. (2009) 'This isn't an abstract problem. Targets can kill'. *The Observer,* 22 March 2009.

Cave, E. & Wilkinson, C. (1997) Developing managerial capabilities, in Kydd, L., Crawford, M. & Riches, C. *Professional development for educational management.* Buckingham: Open University, pp.87–95.

Cayton, H. (2004) Some thoughts on medical professionalism and regulation. Paper given to the Royal College of Physicians Working Party on Medical Professionalism, 12 November.

Churches, R. & West-Burnham, J. (2008) Leading learning through relationships: The implications of Neuro-linguistic programming for personalisation and the children's agenda in England. Reading: CfBT Education Trust.

—(2009) Leading learning through relationships: The implications of neuro-linguistic programming for personalisation and the Children's Agenda in England in Tosey, P. (ed.) *Current Research in NLP vol. 1: Proceedings of 2008 Conference.* South Mimms, Herts: ANLP.

Clarkson, R., & Sainsbury, M. (2007) *Children's Attitudes to Reading.* NFER.

Claxton, G. (2008) *What's the point of school? Rediscovering the Heart of Education.* Oxford: Oneworld Publications.

Coffield, F. (1998) (ed.) *Learning at Work.* Bristol: The Policy Press.

Coffield, F., Moseley, D., Hall, E. & Ecclestone, K. (2004) *Learning styles and pedagogy in post-16 learning: A systematic and critical review.* London: Learning and Skills Research Centre.

Collfield, F. & Edward, S. (2009) 'Rolling out "good", "best", and "excellent" practice. What next? Perfect practice?' *British Educational Research Journal,* Vol. 35 No. 3. 371–90.

Conger, J. A., Kanungo, R. N. and Menon, S. T. (2000) 'Charismatic leadership and follower effects'. *Journal of Organizational Behaviour*, 21(7), 747–67.

Cooper, S. (2008) *Brilliant Leaders: What the best leaders know, do and say.* Harlow: Pearson Education, Ltd.

Craft, A. (1999) 'Creative development in the early years: Implications of policy for practice'. *The Curriculum Journal* 10(1), 135–50.

—(2002) Creativity and Early Years Education: A lifewide foundation. London: Continuum International Publishing Group Ltd.

—(2005) Creativity in *Schools: Tensions and Dilemmas.* Abingdon, Oxon: Routledge.

Craft, A. Jeffrey, B. and Leibling, M. (2001) *Creativity in Education.* London and New York: Continuum.

Creemers, B. & Kyriakides, L. (2008) *The dynamics of educational effectiveness.* London: Routledge.

Cropley, A. J. (2001) *Creativity in education and learning: A guide for teachers and educators.* Abingdon, Oxon: Kogan Page, Ltd.

Cruddas, L. (2005) *Learning Mentors in Schools: Policy and Practice.* Stoke on Trent: Trentham Books.

Csikszentmihalyi, M. (1996) *Creativity: Flow and the Psychology of discovery and invention.* New York: HarperCollins.

—(1997) *Finding Flow: The psychology of engagement with everyday life.* New York: Basic Books.

Davies, C. (2009) 'Focus on fact is stifling schools, warns top head'. *The Observer,* 8 March.

Davies, M. (2009) 'Vital to maintain confidence in the teaching profession'. *Western Mail,* 16 April.

Davies, M. & Edwards, G. (2001) 'Will the curriculum caterpillar ever learn to fly?' in Fielding, M. (ed.), *Taking Education Really Seriously: Four Years' Hard Labour.* London: RoutledgeFalmer, pp.96–105.

Dempster, N (2009) 'What do we know about leadership?' in MacBeath, J. & Dempster, N. (eds) *Connecting Leadership and Learning: Principles for Practice.* Abingdon, Oxon: Routledge. pp.20–31.

Dempster, N. and Bagakis, G. (2009) 'An environment for learning (principle 2)', in MacBeath, J. & Dempster, N. (eds) *Connecting Leadership and Learning: Principles for Practice.* Abingdon, Oxon: Routledge, pp.91–105.

Department for Children, Education, Lifelong Learning and Skills (2008a) *School Effectiveness Framework: Building effective learning communities together.* Cardiff: Welsh Assembly Government.

—(2008b) *Transforming Education and Training Provision in Wales: Delivering Skills that Work for Wales.* Cardiff: Welsh Assembly Government.

Department for Education and Skills (2002) *Statistics of Education.*

de Waal, A. cited by Tweedie, N. (2010) 'Bottom of the Class'. *The Daily Telegraph,* 25 February 2010, p.19.

Dilts, R. (1996) *Visionary Leadership Skills: Creating a world to which people want to belong.* Capitola, CA: Meta Publications Inc.

Dragovic, T. (2007) *Teachers' professional identity and the role of CPD in its creation – a report on a study into how NLP and non-NLP trained teachers in Slovenia talk about their professional identity and their work,* International Society for Teacher Education, 27th Annual International Seminar at University of Stirling, Scotland, 24–30 June 2007.

Dunbar, R. (2010) *How Many Friends does One Person Need? Dunbar's Number and Other Evolutionary Quirks*. London: Faber & Faber Ltd.

Dweck, C. (2006) Mindset: The new psychology of success. New York: Random House.

Elliott, A. (2007) *State schools since the 1950s: The good news*. Stoke-on-Trent: Trentham Books.

Elliott, J. G., Stemler, S. E., Sternberg, R. J., Grigorenko, E. L. and Hoffman, N. (2011) 'The socially skilled teacher and the development of tacit knowledge'. *British Educational Research Journal* Vol. 37, No. 1, February, 83–103.

Estyn (2011) *Literacy and the Foundation Phase: An evaluation of the implementation of the Foundation Phase for five to six-year-olds in primary schools with special reference to literacy*. September 2011. Estyn: Her Majesty's Inspectorate for Education and Training in Wales.

Feldman, D. H., Czikszentmihalyi, M. and Gardner, H. (1994) *Changing the World: A Framework for the Study of Creativity*. Westport, CT and London: Praeger.

Fiedler, F. R., Chemers, M. M. & Mahar, I. (1977) *Improving Leadership Effectiveness: The Leader Match Concept*. New York: John Wiley.

Fisher, R. (2005) Teaching Children to Think. Cheltenham: Nelson Thornes Ltd.

Flaherty, J. (2005) *Coaching: Evoking excellence in others* (2nd Edition). Oxford: Elsevier Butterworth-Heinemann.

Fullan, M. (2004) *System Thinkers in Action: Moving beyond the Standards Plateau*. London/Nottingham: DfES Innovation Unit / NCSL.

—(2008) *The Six Secrets of Change: What the Best Leaders Do to Help Their Organizations Survive and Thrive*. San Francisco: Jossey-Bass.

Galbraith, J. K. (1996) *The Good Society: The Humane Agenda*. London: Reed International Books Ltd.

Gardner, H. (1983) *Frames of Mind*. London: Fontana Press.

Gardner, H., Csikszentmihalyi, M. & Damon, W. (2001) *Good Work: When Excellence and Ethics Meet*. New York: Basic Books.

George, B., (2003) *Authentic leadership: Rediscovering the secrets to creating lasting value*. San Francisco, CA: Josey-Bass.

George, B., Sims, P., McLean, A. N. and Mayer, D. (2007) 'Discovering your authentic leadership'. *Harvard Business Review*, February, 129–38.

Gerver, R. (2010) *Creating Tomorrow's Schools Today: Education – Our Children, Their Futures*. London & New York: Continuum International Publishing Group.

Gladwell, M. (2000) *The Tipping Point: How little things can make a big difference*. London: Abacus.

—(2008) *Outliers: The Story of Success*. London: Penguin Books.

Goleman, D. (1996) *Emotional Intelligence: Why it can matter more than IQ*. London: Bloomsbury Publishing plc.

—(1998) *Working with Emotional Intelligence*. London: Bloomsbury Publishing plc.

—(2002) *The New Leaders: Emotional Intelligence at Work*. London: Little, Brown.

Gould, S. J. (1981) *The mismeasure of man*. New York: W. W. Norton.

Griffith, R. (2000) *National Curriculum: National disaster, education and citizenship*. London: Routledge Palmer.

Gudmundsdottir, S. (1990) 'Values in pedagogical content knowledge', *Journal of Teacher Education*, 41: 3: 44–52.

Gundara, J. (2000) 'Social Diversity, Inclusiveness and Citizenship Education', in Lawton, D., Cairns, J. and Gardner, R. (eds) *Education for Citizenship*. London: Continuum, pp.14–25.

Halstead, M. & Taylor, M. J. (1996) *Values in Education and Education in Values*. Abingdon, Oxon: RoutledgeFalmer.

Handy, C. (1993) *Understanding Organizations*. London: Penguin Books.

—(1995) *Beyond Certainty: The Changing World of Organizations*. London: Random House (UK) Ltd.

Hannan, D. (2009) *'My speech to Gordon Brown goes viral'*. Daily Telegraph, 25 March.

Hargreaves, A. (2003) *Teaching in the Knowledge Society: Education in the Age of Insecurity*. Maidenhead: Open University Press.

Hargreaves, A. & Fink, D. (2006) *Sustainable Leadership*. San Francisco: John Wiley & Sons Inc.

Hargreaves, D. (2005) About Learning: Report of the Learning Working Group. London: Demos.

Harris, A. (2009) *'Creative leadership: Developing future leaders'*. Management in Education. British Educational Leadership, Management & Administration Society (BELMAS) Vol 23(1): 9–11.

Hofstede, G. (1984) *Culture's Consequences*. London: Sage Publications.

Hopkins, D. (2009) *The Emergence of System Leadership*. Nottingham: National College for School Leadership.

House, R. J., Hanges, P. J., Javidan, M., Dorfman, P. W., Gupta, V. and GLOBE associates (eds) (2004) *Cultures, Leadership and Organizations: A 62 Nation GLOBE Study*, Vol. 1. Thousand Oaks, CA: Sage.

Hoyle, E. (1986) *The Politics of School Management*. Sevenoaks: Hodder and Stoughton.

Hyman, T. (2009) Drop GCSEs. 'We should be teaching our children to think'. *The Observer,* 16 August.

Illich, I. (1973) *Deschooling Society*. Harmondsworth, Middlesex: Penguin Education.

Jeffrey, B. (ed.) (2006) *Creative learning practices: European experiences*. London: Tuffnell Press.

Jeffrey, B. & Craft, A. (2001) The universalization of creativity in education, in Craft, A., Jeffrey, B. & Leibling, M. (eds) *Creativity in Education*. London: Continuum, pp.1–13.

Jensen, E. (2008) *Brain-based Learning: the New Paradigm of Teaching* (2nd Edition). Thousand Oaks, Cal: Corwin Press.

Kavanagh, M. H. & Ashkanasy, N. M. (2006) 'The Impact of Leadership and Change Management Strategy on Organizational Culture and Individual Acceptance of Change during a Merger'. *British Journal of Management,* Vol. 17. S81-S.103.

Kelly, A. & Hall, J. (2009) *We should develop collaboration between teachers, schools and sectors*, in Lessons from the Front 2009. London: A Policy First Publication, Chapter 2

Kennedy, H, QC (1998) A Self-Perpetuating Learning Society: A Report on Participation in Further Education, in Ranson, S. (ed.) *Inside the Learning Society*. London: Cassell Education, pp. 163–69.

Kidger, J., Gunnell, D., Biddle, L., Campbell, R. and Donovan, J. (2010) 'Part and parcel of teaching? Secondary school staff's views on supporting student emotional health and well-being' *British Educational Research Journal*, Vol. 36, No.6, 919–35.

Kinder, K. (1997) 'Causes of disaffection: the views of pupils and educational professionals'. *EERA Bulletin* 3 (1), 3–11.

Knight, S. (1995) *NLP at Work: The difference that makes the difference in business.* London: Nicholas Brealey Publishing.

Korthagen, F. A. J. (2004) 'In search of the essence of a good teacher', *Teaching and Teacher Education*, 20: 1: 77–97.

Kragh, G. (1995) Education for Democracy, Social Justice, Respect for Human Rights and Global Responsibility: a psychological perspective, in Osler, A., Rathenow, H-F. & Starkey, H. (eds) *Teaching for Citizenship in Europe.* Stoke-on-Trent: Trentham Books, pp.41–5. Kydd, L. (1997) Teacher professionalism and managerialism, in Kydd, L., Crawford, M. & Riches, C. *Professional development for educational management.* Buckingham: Open University Press, pp.111–17.

Laborde, G. Z. (1998) *Influencing with Integrity: Management skills for communication and negotiation.* Carmarthen: Crown House Publishing.

Lee, T-P (2007) Using systems Thinking to Improve Organizational Learning in the Public Sector: Perspective of Public Officials. http//:www.systemdynamics. org/conferences.2007/proceed/papers.LEE155pdf.

MacBeath, J. (2009) A focus on learning (principle 1), in MacBeath, J. Dempster, N. (eds). *Connecting Leadership and Learning: Principles for Practice.* Abingdon, Oxon. & New York: Routledge, pp.74–90.

MacMurray, J. (1961) *Persons in Relation.* London: Faber & Faber.

McWilliam, E. & Haukka, S. (2008) 'Educating the creative workforce: new directions for twenty-first century schooling'. *British Educational Research Journal,* Vol. 34 No. 5, 651–66.

Mintzberg, H. (2004) *Managers not MBAs.* San Francisco: Berrett-Koehler.

Monbiot, G. (2002) 'What do we really want?' *The Guardian,* 27 August.

Morgan, G. (1997) *Images of Organization.* Thousand Oaks: Sage.

Mortimore, P. (2009) 'Let's end these crackpot schemes'. *The Guardian – Education,* 7 April, p.4.

Muijs, D. & Lindsay, G. (2008) 'Where are we at? An empirical study of levels and methods of evaluating continuing professional development'. *British Educational Research Journal,* Vol. 34 No.2, 195–211

Mumford, M. D., Scott, G. M., Gaddis, & B., Strange, J. M. (2002) 'Leading creative people: Orchestrating expertise and relationships'. *The Leadership Quarterly,* 13, 705–50.

National Assembly for Wales (2004) Learning Pathways 14–19 Guidance Circular No. 37/2004. Cardiff: Welsh Assembly Government.

National College for School Leadership (2009) *Developing Outstanding Leaders: Professional Life Histories of Outstanding Headteachers.* Summary Report

Northouse, P. G. (2004) Leadership: Theory and practice. London: Sage

O'Connor, J. (1998) Leading with NLP: Essential leadership skills for influencing and managing people. London: Thorsons.

O'Connor, J. & McDermott, I. (1997) The Art of Systems Thinking: Essential skills for creativity and problem solving. London: Thorsons.

OECD (2010) *PISA 2009 Results; What Makes a School Successful (Volume IV).*

Ogawa, R. T. & Bossert, S. T. (1997) 'Leadership as an organizational quality', in Crawford, M., Kydd, L. & Riches, C. (eds) *Leadership and teams in educational management*. Buckingham: Open University Press, pp.9–21.

Orenstein, Ruth, I. (2006) 'Measuring Executive Coaching Efficacy? The Answer was right here all the time'. *Consulting Psychology Journal: Practice and Research,* Vol. 58 No. 2, 106–116.

Oscarsson, V. (1995) 'Pupils' Views of the Future', in Osler, A., Rathenow, H-F. & Starkey, H. (eds) *Teaching for Citizenship in Europe*. Stoke-on-Trent: Trentham Books, pp.201–216.

Pachier, N., Daly, C. and Lambert, D. (2003) 'Teacher learning: Reconceptualising the relationship between theory and practical teaching in masters level course development', *Proceedings: Forum for Quality Assurance in Distance-Learning,* University of London: Institute of Education.

Pfeffer, J. & Sutton, R. I. (2006) *Hard facts, dangerous half-truths and total nonsense: Profiting from evidence-based management*. Boston: Harvard Business School Press.

Pinker, S. (2002) *The Blank Slate: The Modern Denial of Human Nature.* London: The Penguin Press.

Pollard. A. (2009) Education Lecture (31 March), General Teaching Council for Northern Ireland, .

Pring, R., Hayward, G., Hadgson, A., Johnson, J., Keep, E., Oances, A., Rees, G., Spours, K. & Wilde, S. (2009) *Education for All: The Future of Education and Training for 14–19 year olds*. Oxford: University of Oxford.

Qualifications & Curriculum Authority (1998) *Education for citizenship and the teaching of democracy in schools: Final report of the Advisory Group on Citizenship*. London: QCA.

Reeves, R. (2001) *Happy Mondays: Putting the pleasure back into work*. Harlow: Pearson Educational Ltd.

—(2007) John Stuart Mill: Victorian Firebrand. London: Atlantic Books.

Richardson, K. and Allnut, J. (2009) 'We should nurture teachers' inquisitiveness', in Lessons from the Front. Teach First: A Teach First Ambassador Publication, pp.20–3.

Ritzer, G. F. (2011) *The McDonaldisation of Society 6*. London: Sage Publications Ltd.

Robinson, Sir K. (2001) *Out of our Minds: Learning to be Creative*. Chichester: Capstone Publishing Ltd.

—(2006) Schools kill Creativity. *http://www.ted.com/index.php/talks/ken_robinson*. Accessed 18 May 2009.

Robson, J. & Bailey, B. (2009), '"Bowing from the heart": an investigation into discourses of professionalism and the work of caring for students in further education'. *British Educational Research Journal*, Vol. 35, No.1, February 2009, 99–117.

Roycroft-Davis C. (2010) 'A self-made man'. *Daily Express,* Thursday 10 June.

Runco, M. A. (2004) 'Everyone has creative potential', in Sternberg, R. J., Grigorenko, E. L. and Singer, J. L. *Creativity: From Potential to Realization*. Washington DC: American Psychological Association, pp.21–30.

Ryan, W. (author) & Gilbert, I. (editor) (2008) *Leadership with a Moral Purpose: Leading your school inside out*. Carmarthen: Crown House Publishing.

Sachs, J. (2003) *The Activist Teaching Profession*. Buckingham: Open University Press.

Sammons, P., Thomas, S. and Mortimore, P. (1997) *Forging Links: Effective Schools and Effective Departments.* London: Paul Chapman Publishing.

Scott, J. C. (1998) *Seeing like a state: How certain schemes to improve the human condition have failed.* New Haven CT: Yale University Press.

Seldon, A. & James, D. (2009) 'A-levels should be replaced with a system that has integrity'. *The Independent,* 14 July.

Senge, P. M. (1990) *The Fifth Discipline: The Art and Practice of The Learning Organization.* London: Century Business.

Senge, P., Scharmer, C. O., Jawarski, J. & Flowers, B. S. (2004) *Presence.* Cambridge, MA: Society of Organizational Learning.

Sennett, R. (2010) 'May the asbo rest in peace'. *The Guardian,* 31 July p.26.

Sergiovanni, T. (2005) *Strengthening the Heartbeat.* San Francisco: Jossey Bass.

Shah, S. (2006) 'Education leadership: an Islamic perspective'. *British Educational Research Journal* Vol. 32, No. 3 (June), pp.363–85.

Solomon, R. C. & Flores, F. (2001) Building Trust: in Business, Politics, Relationships and Life. New York: Oxford University Press.

Spreitzer, G., McCall, M. & Mahoney, J. D. (1997) 'Early identification of international executive potential'. *Journal of Applied Psychology* 82, 6–29.

Sternberg, R. (ed.) (1999) *Handbook of creativity.* Cambridge: Cambridge University Press.

Sternberg, R. J. (2005) 'A model of educational leadership: Wisdom, intelligence, and creativity, synthesized'. *International Journal of Leadership in Education,* Oct-Dec Vol. 8 No. 4, 347–64.

Sutton, M. (1997) 'Allocating budgets for curriculum support' in Preedy, M., Glatter, R. and Levacic, R. *Educational Management: Strategy, quality and resources.* Buckingham: Open University Press, pp.160–70.

Swann, M., McIntyre, D., Pell, T., Hargreaves, L. & Cunningham, M. (2010) 'Teachers' conceptions of teacher professionalism in England in 2003 and 2006'. *British Educational Research Journal* Vol. 36 No. 4 (August) pp.549–71.

Taylor, J., Roehig, A. D., Soden Hensler, B., Connor, C. M., & Schatschneider, C. (2010) 'Teacher Quality Moderates the Genetic Effects of Early Reading'. *Science,* Vol. 328, No. 5977 23 April, pp.512—214.

The Princes Trust (2007) *The Cost of Exclusion: Counting the Cost of Youth Disadvantage in the UK.* London: The Princes Trust with the Centre for Economic Performance, London School of Economics.

Thomas, G. (2009) 'What works' as a Sublinguistic Grunt, with Lessons from Catachresis, Asymptote, Football and Pharma.' *Research intelligence: News from the British Educational Research Association,* Issue 106, March 2009, pp.20–2.

Thomas, P. (2010) *Ban the Boss.* BBC 1 Wales. Wednesday 17 March.

Trowler, P. (2002) *Education Policy: A policy sociology approach* (2nd Edition). London: RoutledgeFalmer.

Turnbull, J. & Beese, J. (2000) 'Negotiating the Boundaries: the experience of the mental health nurse at the interface with the criminal justice system'. *Journal of Psychiatric and Mental Health Nursing* 7: 289–96.

Turnbull, J. (2002) 'Values in Educating for Citizenship: sources, influences and assessment'. *Pedagogy, Culture and Society,* Vol. 10, No.1, 123–34

—(2007) 9 Habits of Highly Effective Teachers. London: Continuum International Publishing Group.

—(2009) *Coaching for Learning: A Practical Guide for Encouraging Learning*. London: Continuum International Publishing Group.

Turner, D. (2010) *Using the Medical Model in Education: Can pills make you clever?* London: Continuum International Publishing Group Ltd.

Tweedie, N. (2010) 'Bottom of the Class'. *The Daily Telegraph*, 25 February.

UNESCO (2001) Cultural heritage, creativity and education for all. Paris: Division of the Arts and Cultural Enterprises, Sector of Culture, United Nations Educational, Scientific and Cultural Organisation.

Weindling, D. (1997) 'Strategic planning in schools: some practical techniques', in Preedy, M., Glatter, R. & Levacic, R. *Educational Management: Strategy, quality and resources*. Buckingham: Open University Press, pp.218–33.

Welshman, S. (2006) Enterprise is the key to the future. *Australian Higher Education Supplement* 11 January 2007.

West-Burnham, J. (2009) *Rethinking Education Leadership: From improvement to transformation*. London & New York: Continuum International Publishing Group.

West-Burnham, J., Farrar, M. and Otero, G. (2007) *Schools and Communities: Working Together to Transform Children's Lives*. London: Network Continuum Education.

West-Burnham, J. & Ireson, J. (2005) *Leadership Development and Personal Effectiveness*. Nottingham: NCSL

White, J. (1998) *Do Howard Gardner's multiple intelligences add up?* London: Institute of Education University of London.

Whitmore, J. (2002) *Coaching for Performance: GROWing People, Performance and Purpose* (3rd Edition). London & Boston: Nicholas Brearley Publishing.

Wilby, P. (2010) 'The Profile: Disciple of discipline'. *The Guardian* – Education, 5 January 2010.

Wilson, J. (2000) *Key Issues in Education and Teaching*. London: Cassell

Wood, D. (1998) *How Children Think and Learn* (2nd Edition). Oxford: Blackwell Publishers Ltd.

Index